ARTHUR QUILLER-COUCH

Q, *from the portrait by*
Sir William Nicholson

ARTHUR QUILLER-COUCH

A biographical study of

Q

BY F. BRITTAIN, M.A.

Fellow of Jesus College
Cambridge

CAMBRIDGE: AT THE UNIVERSITY PRESS
NEW YORK: THE MACMILLAN COMPANY

1948

TO

LADY QUILLER-COUCH

CONTENTS

PREFACE

Q often asserted that he would never write his autobiography but was persuaded to change his mind and so began his *Memories and Opinions*. He died, however, when he had covered only the first twenty-four years of his life—that is to say, the period from 1863 to 1887.

In order to make my narrative complete, it was necessary for me to begin at the beginning. I have, however, been brief up to the year 1887, though I have filled some gaps that Q left, mostly through modesty. I have gone into greater detail from the year 1887 onwards.

I have tried to write as objectively as possible, even though I knew Q intimately. My rooms at Jesus College were on the floor above his, and my feelings towards him were such that I spent as much time in his company as I could.

I hope I have made it clear that certain persistent legends that are told about Q are without foundation. To leave no room for doubt, I state here that he was not in T. E. Brown's house at Clifton, never met R. L. Stevenson, was never a candidate for Parliament, was not the first King Edward VII Professor of English Literature at Cambridge and did not make the remarks ending with 'There's no hurry: the ship doesn't sail till next week' (or words to that effect). These remarks have been ascribed to many lecturers in many universities. It is uncertain how old they are. What is certain is that Q did not make them and could not have made them.

I wish to thank all those who helped me by lending letters or in other ways. My thanks are due especially to Lady Quiller-Couch, Miss Quiller-Couch, Mrs Symondson, Dr H. F. Stewart, Miss Eleanor Reid, Miss Dorothy Hern, Mr S. C. Roberts, Sir Sydney Cockerell, Mr Vincent Robinson, the Hon. Gilbert Coleridge,

Preface

Miss Isobel Keith, Mrs Mary Hicks, General Sir Henry Jackson, K.C.B., Miss Mary Kelly, the Rev. Austin Lee, Sir Richard Luce, the Misses F. G. and M. G. Nixon, Miss S. Weston, Miss R. Philpott, Mr L. L. Price, Canon J. G. Tuckey, Mr R. A. J. Walling, the Misses Tyacke, Mr Gerald Bullett, all those (mentioned on p. xi) who gave me permission to use illustrations of which they own the copyright and to Lady Cynthia Asquith for permission to include some extracts from Sir James Barrie's letters to Q.

The bibliography printed at the end of this book shows the vast extent and very wide range of Q's writings. No representative selection from them has ever been published. I am compiling one now for publication by Messrs J. M. Dent and Sons.

F. B.

March 1947

'C' Staircase, First Court,
Jesus College, Cambridge

LIST OF ILLUSTRATIONS

CHAPTER I

EARLY YEARS (1863–82)

ARTHUR QUILLER-COUCH, commonly called 'Q' from the pseudonym that he used in his writings, was descended on his father's side from two Cornish families —the Quillers and the Couches. Both families had lived for generations at Polperro, a striking fishing village in the parish of Talland on the south coast of Cornwall. No one who has once seen Polperro, with its diminutive harbour almost hidden from the sea, its lines of fishing-boats and its close-packed houses clinging to the sides of a narrow ravine, can ever forget it. Nor is it easy to forget Talland on its hill a mile away, with its beautiful barrel-roofed church, its ancient carved pews, its monuments to the Beville and Grenville families, and its bell-tower around which the sea-birds ceaselessly wheel and cry.

The Couches have probably been settled in Cornwall from time immemorial. Their name is said to be a variant of the Cornish word *coch*, meaning 'red', and is pronounced 'Cooch'. When anyone—as often happened—asked Q how it should be pronounced he sometimes answered: 'Not like a sofa.' His scout at Oxford was once overheard saying to his assistant: 'Here, take this to Mr Cowch, but don't let him hear you call him "Mr Cowch".'

The Couches appear to have been originally yeoman farmers but by the eighteenth century were drawing their living from the sea. One of the family fought at Trafalgar. Another died with Sir John Franklin in the Arctic in 1847. Q's great-grandfather, Richard Couch, abandoned seafaring and became a fish merchant at Polperro, where he prospered. His only child, Jonathan Couch, who was born in 1789, broke away from family tradition by becoming a doctor and practised in his native Polperro. Like his immediate ancestors, he was a staunch Methodist. We catch many glimpses of him, of his love of ichthyology, and of his village (under the name of Polpier or Polpeor) in his grandson's writings.

I

He figures in *Corporal Sam and Other Stories*, for instance, as 'Doctor Unonius', whose education had been partly paid for by his father's smuggling expeditions. Q remembered seeing his grandfather once only but always had the greatest respect and affection for his memory.

Jonathan Couch married three times, his second wife being Jane Quiller, whom he married in 1815. The Quillers were said to be of French origin but had lived at Polperro for five generations at least and were a seafaring family. One of them is reputed to have led five hundred smuggling expeditions without incurring a single casualty among his men.

Q doubtless had both Couches and Quillers in mind when he wrote

> By Talland Church as I did go
> I passed my kindred all in a row,
>
> Straight and silent there by the spade
> Each in his narrow chamber laid.

The gravestones of one or two Quillers can certainly be seen in the precipitous churchyard at Talland and no doubt others lie there in unnamed graves. Yet there are fewer members of the family buried at Talland than there should be, for many of them died at sea—Jane Quiller's father and all the rest of her male relations among them. When, therefore, she married Jonathan Couch she and her husband had no need to look for a house but continued to live in her old home. It still stands and is known as 'Couch's house', though no Couch has lived in it since Jonathan died in 1870.

Jonathan and Jane Couch had six children, to four of whom their mother's family name was given as a second baptismal name. Five of the six children were boys and three of them became doctors. One of these, Thomas Quiller Couch, settled down to practise medicine at the small town of Bodmin, which lies about ten miles from the south coast of Cornwall and about the same distance from the north coast. He married Mary Ford, of the Devonshire village of Abbotskerswell near Newton Abbot, and lived at 63 Fore Street, Bodmin, until his death in 1884. The house stands opposite a Methodist chapel but the Methodist ministers who succeeded each other there did not consult Dr Couch when they wanted medical advice. They liked to have a doctor of their own religious persuasion; and Thomas Couch, whether from conviction or because his wife and all her family were Anglicans, had by this time conformed to the Church of England, with the result that his five children were brought up Anglicans. The eldest of the five, Arthur Thomas Quiller Couch—he did not adopt the hyphen until 1889—was born at his parents' home on 21 November 1863 and baptized in Bodmin parish church on Twelfth Day 1864. He was confirmed during his school days and many years later he wrote: 'The bishop who confirmed me must have been kindness itself: for he came from Zululand—yes, 'faith, all the way—and he had long side-whiskers and—well, you've seen the result.'

Q was half Devonian by blood, for his mother's family had been settled in South Devon for generations. The Devonian element in him was strengthened by seven years spent in the county as a schoolboy at Newton Abbot College, a 'School for the Sons of Gentlemen'. Walter Shaw Sparrow, who was a pupil there at the same time as Q, says that 'Newton was not at all snobbish, but her atmosphere was like that of one of the very private schools which are called public; indeed, she was a *new* public school, and eager to make a name in sports, games, scholarship, and the professions'. When Q entered the school he was (as he himself put it) 'an ugly little red-haired urchin of ten'. Shaw Sparrow describes him as 'a small and stout fellow with a thick mass of sandy hair and a face wonderfully covered with variegated freckles'. He continues: 'He absorbed Greek and Latin as a sponge drinks water and was never in a hurry and never ill-tempered. I don't remember him as a player of games, but he would defend himself against all comers, his tongue whipping banter and satire, while his face puckered into grins'. For the first two years Q was a day-boy, living with his mother's parents, who since his infancy had moved the short distance from Abbotskerswell to the town of Newton Abbot. The headmaster, after Q's first year at the school, was the Reverend George Townsend Warner, whom he afterwards described as 'a gentleman with every attribute of a good headmaster save a sense of justice, of which he had scarcely a glimmer'. Q's chief scholastic rival was the headmaster's elder son, George, who (like Q) ultimately became a Fellow of Jesus College, Cambridge, though he left Cambridge long before Q arrived there.

Q spent his school holidays with his parents at Bodmin and from it explored the surrounding country. It was in the late summer of 1879 that he first made his way southward down the River Fowey and visited the little port of Fowey itself. He found it very charming and stayed there for some time, in lodgings overlooking the harbour. More than sixty years later, in his *Memories and Opinions*, he recalled his first evening in the town to which he later became so intensely attached:

That night before undressing I stood long and gazed on the harbour, the track of the moon on its water, the riding lights of two or three small schooners at anchor in the shadow of the farther shore, and decided that this were no bad place in which to live. And that is all I need say here of my first acquaintance with the upper and lower reaches of an estuary the tides of which time has since woven so close into the pulse of my own life that memory cannot now separate the rhythms.

It was probably during this visit to Fowey that he first met the lady who was to be his wife.

By this time Thomas Couch, with five children to educate, was finding increasing difficulty in making ends meet. It was perhaps for that reason that his eldest son, though already sixteen years old, decided to try for a scholarship at one of the big public schools— one with more endowment than Newton Abbot, which had very little. He wanted to try for Winchester, but his headmaster forgot to enter his name in time for the examination. He therefore tried for Clifton, was successful, and went into residence at the school in the autumn of 1880.

Clifton College, Bristol, had grown rapidly since its foundation in 1862 and during Q's two years of residence it had nearly seven hundred boys. Among them were those who afterwards became well known as Field-Marshal Lord Birdwood, Sir Francis Younghusband, Sir Henry Newbolt and John M'Taggart, the philosopher. Sir Richard Luce, who was Q's fag, wrote sixty-five years later:

As a small boy in Dakyns's House at Clifton in 1880 I well remember Couch's arrival there. He was considered by us as somewhat of a phenomenon, for he had as a new boy been placed directly into the Sixth Form; as far as my knowledge goes, the only case on record. He was naturally regarded by us small boys with considerable suspicion.

One recollection I have vividly in mind concerning him. It must have been in September 1881, after the summer term, during which top hats were laid aside and only straws were worn. On opening the box to extract his Sunday hat he found it occupied by a nest of young mice. My memory of his face when he showed it to us is that it was filled with disgust rather than with amusement or scientific interest.

In his first year at Clifton Q won the school prize for an original English poem on a set theme—Athens. His chief rival for the prize was Henry Newbolt, who long afterwards remembered feeling more disappointed than surprised at his defeat. Q's verses were published in the school magazine, *The Cliftonian*, in July 1881 and his parents afterwards had them reprinted as a booklet at Bodmin. This first publication of one who was to write so much about the sea opens appropriately with a seascape:

As some shattered piece of wreckage, in the waste of ocean lost,
Floats and drifts in aimless motion, on the heaving billows tosst,
Now amid the boiling eddies, now upon the foaming crest;
Hither, thither, rising, plunging, in a blind and vague unrest:
So our souls are tossed and driven o'er the trackless depths of sleep,
Lifted now in dreams to heaven, now engulfed within the deep.

Q came to know Bristol better than most of his fellow-Cliftonians, partly because he had relatives in the city and partly because he edited *The Cliftonian* for a time. Edward Gustavus Clarke, the Official Receiver in Bankruptcy at Bristol, was his mother's first cousin. Like his young relative, he was a generous, hospitable man with a keen sense of humour. Q found his company very congenial and spent much time at his house, particularly at week-ends. As editor of *The Cliftonian* Q naturally came into frequent contact with the publisher of the magazine, J. W. Arrowsmith, who had a great love for Bristol and an extensive knowledge of the city and its history. He became Q's life-long friend and later published half a dozen of his books, from *The Westcotes* to *Mortallone*, which has Bristol for its background.

Q's school-days came to an end in July 1882. In the following October, when he was nearly nineteen, he went into residence at Trinity College, Oxford, with an entrance scholarship in Classics that he had won during the previous spring.

CHAPTER II

OXFORD (1882-87)

Q SPENT his first year at Oxford in lodgings and then moved into Cardinal Newman's old rooms at Trinity. He made his mark in the College from the beginning, both with the seniors and with the undergraduates. He was excellent company, being widely read for his age, witty, humorous and quick at repartee. Always cautious in making friends, he nevertheless had a great capacity for friendship and was intensely loyal to anyone who became his friend. He appealed to both scholars and athletes, being equally good at reading a literary paper to the Gryphon Club, at handling an oar and at coaching a boat. Rowing was by far his favourite recreation at Oxford. He rowed in the Trinity first boat and ultimately succeeded his rowing mentor, Gilbert Coleridge, as captain of the College boat club.

His chief extravagance in his undergraduate days was in his dress. Fond of bright colours all his life, he had been noted even at Clifton for his gay waistcoats and on his very first day there had been publicly chidden by his house-master for the brilliance of his window-curtains—a snub which clouded his happy memories of Clifton as long as he lived. At Trinity he was famous for his very loud check suits, and the President himself is said to have greeted him one day with: 'What! *another* new pair of *trarsers*, Mr Couch?'

Although his social activities and his rowing occupied a great deal of his time he took a first class in Classical Moderations at the end of his second year. At the beginning of his third year, in October 1884, his University career nearly came to a sudden end owing to the death of his father, who left little or no provision for his widow and children. It seemed at first that the eldest son would have to leave Oxford at once and earn something to support the family. Fortunately, however, Mrs Couch's father, Elias Ford, came to the rescue and enabled him to stay on at Oxford. Q hoped —and his grandfather shared the hope—that he would do well enough in his final examination to be elected a Fellow of his College and stay at Oxford for good.

In October 1885 Charles Cannan, a young Fellow of Trinity and probably the closest friend Q ever had, accepted the editorship of *The Oxford Magazine* on the understanding that Q would help him. This periodical—a University weekly founded in 1883 and already well established—was intended for seniors rather than undergraduates and kept a high literary standard. Q more than fulfilled his promise to Cannan, for his contributions to *The Oxford Magazine* included some of the best verse he ever wrote. Among them were those burlesques of standard English poets which, reprinted in 1893 in his collection of light verse called *Green Bays*, give him a high place among modern parodists. His life-long practice of signing his writings with the one letter 'Q' began with these contributions to *The Oxford Magazine*.

He contributed not merely to what *The Isis* in its first issue (in 1892) called 'the Scylla of the *Magazine's* monotony', but also to what it called 'the Charybdis of the *Rattle's* rollickings'. *The Rattle* was a short-lived occasional paper which appeared for six days a year during the Torpids of 1886 and 1887 and the Eights of 1888. Q edited the first volume and in order to get its last issue out on the appointed day he found it necessary to write the whole of it himself between 7.30 and midnight the previous evening.

In the summer of 1886 he sat for the final examination for his degree and this time was awarded only a second class. Literary, social and athletic activities had taken up so much of his time that he can be excused for not having done better. His comparative failure was nevertheless a great blow to him; for although the President and Fellows of Trinity immediately appointed him to a College lectureship it was clear that they would not elect him to the Fellowship for which he had hoped.

A second blow followed very closely on the first. He had spent part of each summer vacation at Fowey ever since his first visit; and he was at Fowey once more when he was summoned to Plymouth by his grandfather, who informed him that he had incurred such financial losses that he could no longer support anyone but himself. Q accepted without a murmur (except one of compassion for his grandfather) the grave responsibility which he realized had fallen on his own shoulders—the responsibility of supporting not merely himself and his mother but also (until they were old enough to keep themselves) his two brothers and two sisters. He not merely accepted the situation, but even went back to Fowey with a feeling of reckless confidence in himself. What immediately followed can be told only in his own words, taken from his *Memories and Opinions*:

That same evening I asked the lady of my affection to be my wife. It was mad no doubt. It would have been wicked had I not started by making a clean breast of the odds against me. Let it be enough to say here that, as I write, looking back over fifty-odd years, I can declare that hour the most fortunate of my life. We had halted half-way in a short lane leading up from the sea and beside a low wall coped by a quantity of wild thyme, on a tuft of which I rested a hand as I spoke and waited for her answer. To this day, halting before a tuft of the plant I press it and it recalls that answer in its fragrance.

In order to earn a little money immediately, he took a holiday tutorship at Petworth in Sussex for the rest of the Long Vacation. While he was there he began to write his first novel, *Dead Man's Rock*. In the autumn he was back at Trinity, lecturing on Virgil and Aristophanes and at times relieving the monotony of written work for his pupils by setting them passages from Aristophanes to be translated into the West Country dialect. They found him a stimulating lecturer, painstaking and considerate—so considerate that on one occasion (it is said) a notice appeared on his lecture-room door: 'As the University is playing Lancashire this morning there will be no lecture on Herodotus.'

During the Easter vacation of 1887, when staying in a Cumberland farmhouse, he finished *Dead Man's Rock*. He sent it to Cassell's, the London firm who had done well by publishing Stevenson's *Treasure Island* in 1882 and Rider Haggard's *King Solomon's Mines* in 1885. Q's book, which obviously belonged to the same genus as those two classical adventure stories, was accepted. It appeared first in instalments, as a supplement to

Cassell's Saturday Journal. Late that summer, when the author was once more tutoring George O'Brien Wyndham at Petworth, it was published in book form.

The title of *Dead Man's Rock* suited the book admirably. It was the first example of Q's remarkable flair, which he never lost, for inventing book-titles. Hardly one of his thirty-odd volumes of fiction has a title that can be called commonplace.

Dead Man's Rock had a very large sale and gave Q a good start as a writer of fiction but was never a favourite with its author. After re-reading it forty years later he wrote: 'I have been amazed many times—to misquote the great Clive—at my own immoderation.' It is certainly over-written in places but it is an absorbing tale. On the title-page the author appeared merely as 'Q'. There was much speculation about his identity, especially in a review in *Punch* in the autumn of 1887, which said:

Have Messrs Louis Stevenson and Rider Haggard combined under the signature of 'Q' to write at all events the first part of the weird and exciting Romance entitled *Dead Man's Rock*? If not, let those two authors look to their laurels. There is much in this book to remind the reader of *Treasure Island*, especially the fiendish Sailor's uncouth chaunt, 'Sing hey for the deadman's eyes, my lads', which, however, is not a patch upon Mr Stevenson's 'Yo! Ho! Ho! and a bottle of rum' in *Treasure Island*. Then there is one line in 'Q's' story, 'And here a strange thing happened', which must call to mind Mr Rider Haggard's patent of 'and now a strange thing happened'. 'Q'-rious coincidence, isn't it? But a 'coincidence' is not likely to annoy Mr Haggard.

In the first part the most impatient reader will find that he cannot afford to skip a couple of lines without detriment to the narrative, but in the second part he may skip handfuls....

So the summing up is that the first part is first-rate, and the second part is, on the whole, second-rate. But who is 'Q'? That is the Q. and what is the A.?

By the time this review appeared the author of *Dead Man's Rock* had left Oxford and had (he imagined) abandoned the academical life for good. He tells us in his *Memories and Opinions* that he left Oxford for London because he had determined that if he was capable of winning fame in any way he would win it as a writer. There was, however, an over-riding reason for his change of career. Out of sheer modesty he says nothing about this in *Memories and Opinions* or in any of his other writings. Hardly anyone knew of it during his lifetime, but justice to his memory demands that something should be said about it now.

He had discovered that his father had left considerable debts; and, although he was under no obligation to pay them, he felt in honour bound to do so. We may surmise that these debts were due partly to his mother's extravagance, which he mentions more than once in *Memories and Opinions*. They were also partly due, perhaps, to the combined generosity and carelessness of his father, who was clearly more interested in books and natural history than in collecting his patients' fees. Whatever the origin of the parental debts, Q evidently decided that he had a better chance of repaying them by working in London as a writer than by staying at Oxford as a college lecturer without a Fellowship.

Six years later, after working almost day and night with his pen and coming very near a permanent breakdown, he was able to write to a friend: 'I've just paid off the last batch of the family debt; so that, although poor, I feel honest. Think of it! Except once (for a funeral) my head hasn't been inside a top hat for twenty months.'

Nine years after leaving Oxford he contributed to *The Oxford Magazine* one of the best things he ever wrote. Even if all his other writings should be forgotten in the course of time, his *Alma Mater* will be remembered—not merely by Oxonians, but by anyone who knows what it is to be devoted to an institution. Many competent and even admirable poems have been written about seats of learning, but none of them can surpass *Alma Mater* in depth of restrained feeling:

> Know you her secret none can utter?
>   Hers of the Book, the tripled Crown?
> Still on the spire the pigeons flutter;
>   Still by the gateway haunts the gown;
> Still on the street, from corbel and gutter,
>   Faces of stone look down.

Oxford (1882-87)

Faces of stone, and other faces—
    Some from library windows wan
Forth on her gardens, her green spaces,
    Peer and turn to their books anon.
Hence, my Muse, from the green oases
    Gather the tent, begone!

Nay, should she by the pavement linger
    Under the rooms where once she play'd,
Who from the feast would rise and fling her
    One poor *sou* for her serenade?
One poor laugh for the antic finger
    Thrumming a lute-string fray'd?...

Come, old limmer, the times grow colder:
    Leaves of the creeper redden and fall.
Was it a hand then clapp'd my shoulder?
    —Only the wind by the chapel wall.
Dead leaves drift on the lute: so...fold her
    Under the faded shawl.

Never we wince, though none deplore us,
    We, who go reaping that we sow'd;
Cities at cock-crow wake before us—
    Hey, for the lilt of the London road!
One look back and a rousing chorus!
    Never a palinode!

Still on her spire the pigeons hover;
    Still by her gateway haunts the gown.
Ah, but her secret? You, young lover,
    Drumming her old ones forth from town,
Know you the secret none discover?
    Tell it—when *you* go down.

Yet if at length you seek her, prove her,
    Lean to her whispers never so nigh;
Yet if at last not less her lover
    You in your hansom leave the High;
Down from the towers a ray shall hover,
    Touch you—a passer-by!

The man who wrote those lines was obviously in love—deeply in love—with Oxford and he remained so all his life. Although he was destined to be at Cambridge more than six times as long as he had been at Oxford, and although he revelled in life at Cambridge, the feeling was not the same. In 1917, in his *Memoir of Arthur John Butler*, he wrote: 'While a Cambridge man reverts to Cambridge as to a *place*, gracious and hallowed by the feet of great men as well as by those of his own transient youth, it does not lay on him just that spell which binds an Oxford man to *personify* Oxford, to enshrine and adore her as veritably and ineffably, at once and all together, mother and mistress and queen —and yet not three goddesses but one goddess.' Even after a third of a century at Cambridge he still, when he was off his guard, referred to Cambridge men in conversation as 'you' and to Oxford men as 'we'. He spoke of Cambridge with respect, even with enthusiasm; but he spoke of Oxford almost in the same reverent tone that he used when speaking of his wife.

The last issue of *The Oxford Magazine* published during Q's residence in the University contained an imitation of the *Ingoldsby Legends* from his pen. It well expressed the spirit of adventure with which he set out for London:

I laye a-wakynge, and loe! the dawne was breakynge
And rarely pyped a larke for the promyse of the daye:
  'Uppe and sette y^r lance in reste!
  Uppe and followe on the queste!
  Leave the issue to be guessed
    At the endynge of the waye.'

As I lay a-wakynge, 'twas soe she seemed to say:
  'Whatte and if it alle be feynynge?
  There be better thynges than gaynynge,
  Rycher pryzes than attaynynge.'
    And 'twas truthe she seemed to saye.
Whyles the dawne was breakynge, I rode upon my waye.

CHAPTER III

LONDON (1887-92)

WHEN Q left Oxford for London in 1887 he took lodgings at Clareville Grove, Kensington, and worked partly as a free lance but mainly for Cassell's. The chief editor of the firm at this time was John Williams, a former member of Trinity College, Oxford, who befriended Q from the first. In his spare time he guided him round London, imparting, Q said, 'his knowledge of all the haunts and out-of-the-way corners around Fleet Street, Ludgate Hill and "the Row"— a knowledge that ranged from quiet City churches and the halls of guilds with their libraries to the special dishes of uncanny restaurants and wines of recondite cellars'. Some of these peregrinations, especially those to 'uncanny restaurants', were recorded thirty years later in the earlier chapters of Q's *Foe-Farrell*.

Cassell's headquarters were at La Belle Sauvage Yard, Ludgate Hill. The Yard was destroyed in an air-raid during the war of 1939-45, but we get a good description of it from Q's memoir of Arthur Butler, who succeeded John Williams as chief editor of Cassell's in 1892:

Its familiars know it as 'The Yard'; and under that name in my time affectionately blessed or cursed it. It is approached by an archway, the first turning to the left as you go up Ludgate Hill. By the passage, perennially blocked by a carrier's van or vans, you came to the Yard, and at the end of it a door, a stone staircase and a lift with authors upon it, ascending and descending—that is to say, with beings whom you mistook for authors. Later, you learned that they were printers' assistants: still later (from some cynic), that you need not blush for the error—they were probably both.

Narrow tortuous passages ramified from the stone stairway among 'departments' housed in hutches composed of wood and glass. To reach the Editorial Department you took three twists—right, right again, and left—and emerged upon one of several galleries running round a central well, on the floor of which, deep down, the steam-presses laboured in travail with the firm's productions—*The Quiver, Cassell's Saturday Journal, Cassell's Popular Educator, Cassell's Magazine, Chums, Little Folks*, and what not. Their contending din beat on the Chief Editor's door: close outside his window, at the end of the railway bridge stuck—in the late Walter Thornbury's phrase—like a fishbone in the throat of Ludgate Hill, the locomotives of the London, Chatham and Dover Railway Company whistled, shunted, and dallied to blow off steam.

Other corridors wound past 'department' after 'department', into secret places never fully explored by me. There was a counting house, of course; and an Art Department, a Publishing Department, a Publicity Department, a Department (it was rumoured) mysteriously concerned with the laying of eggs, a Department in which Liberal and Conservative scribes wrote leading articles for the provincial press. I shall have more to say about this system of Departments; but the reader will already have remarked in their titles a tendency to 'cross-division'—that error in logic under which Wordsworth classified his poems and an Oxford tradesman advertised himself as 'University, Pork, and Family Butcher'.

Among those who were working for Cassell's at this time was Charles Harrison, the humorous artist. He entertained extensively and at his house Q made many acquaintances and began more than one friendship. It was probably at Harrison's that he first met the artists John Sargent, Francis Millet, Edwin Abbey and Alfred Parsons. Parsons became one of the closest friends of his lifetime and corresponded with him regularly for many years. His other London friends and acquaintances at this time included George Alexander, John Hare, Ellen Terry, Henry James, Joseph Comyns Carr and J. K. Stephen. Stephen consulted him about his short-lived periodical, *The Reflector*—designed, Q said, 'with the double purpose of making a fortune and attacking all the vices of the age'. One event in this London period which stood out in Q's memory in later years was a morning in 1889 which he spent in John Sargent's studio while the artist painted Ellen Terry as Lady Macbeth 'in her green robe of beetles' wings, as she stood in the act of lifting the crown to her brow'. Another outstanding event was a journey which he made with Sargent in the following year to Paris, where they saw Carmencita dance—with the result that Sargent painted his famous portrait of her, now in the Luxembourg. Most of the time, however, Q was working hard with his pen. Some of it was hack work, such as editing for Cassell's a three-volume collection of tales for boys, called *The World of Adventure*. This came out first in monthly parts and was followed a few years later by a similar compilation called *The World of Romance*.

Meanwhile, he was naturally visiting Fowey, the home of his future wife, as often as he could get away from London. His frequent visits to the town, and the enjoyment which he derived from the study of its inhabitants, gave him the inspiration for his second novel, the scene of which he laid at Fowey. The name of the town is pronounced 'Foy'; and in the novel both the name and the town itself were thinly disguised as 'Troy'. *The Oxford English Dictionary* shows that the word 'Troy' had already acquired in English the figurative meaning of 'a scene of disorder or confusion'; and a glossary of terms used in Cornwall, published in 1880, included the expression *Troy town*, which it defined as 'a maze, a labyrinth of streets'.

The Astonishing History of Troy Town, dedicated to Charles Cannan, was published by Cassell's in 1888. It resembles *Dead Man's Rock* in never having been a favourite with its author but is unlike it in almost every other respect. It is true that the element of romance is again present, but farce greatly predominates and it is very entertaining farce. *Troy Town*, with what one of Q's friends aptly called 'its characteristic introduction of the buccaneering spirit into a *Cranford* atmosphere', was one of the best novels he ever wrote, and Admiral Buzza, Miss Limpenny and Caleb Trotter are among the most clearly delineated of all his characters. The book gives a charming picture of an Arcadian past, 'when the young men were not above singing *The Death of Nelson*, or joining in a glee and arming the young ladies home afterwards', when '"Hocken's Slip" had not yet become the

"Victoria Quay" and we talked of the "Rope Walk" where we now say "Marine Parade"'.

Q had barely finished writing *Troy Town* before he set to work on a third novel—*The Splendid Spur*. It was just finished when, on 22 August 1889, he married Miss Louisa Amelia Hicks at Fowey parish church. He was twenty-five at the time. When he was forty he made one of the characters in one of his short stories say: 'In later life a man may seek marriage for its own sake, but at five-and-twenty he marries against his will—because he has fallen in love with a woman.' His was most certainly a love-match. After half a century of married life he was as much in love as he had ever been; and all through that time, whenever he was away from his wife, he never let a day pass without writing to her.

After a brief honeymoon at the Imperial Hotel, Torquay, his wife went to visit some relations in West Cornwall while he set out with Alfred Parsons to follow the course of the Warwickshire Avon from its source near Naseby to its junction with the Severn at Tewkesbury. Their object was to collect material for a book about the Avon, the text of which was to be by Q and the illustrations by Parsons. The first part of the journey was done on foot. At Rugby, where the stream became wide enough, they launched a canoe and finished the expedition by water. *The Warwickshire Avon* is practically unknown to-day but contains a number of good things. Among them is the prose original of Q's well-known *Ode on Eckington Bridge*:

Rain hung over the Malverns; down on the flat plain, where the river crept into the evening, the poplars were swaying gently; a pair of jays hustled by with a warning squawk.

A small discovery awoke us. As we rested our elbows on the parapet, we noticed that many deep grooves or notches ran across it. They were marks worn in the stone by the tow-ropes of departed barges.

Those notches spoke to us, as nothing had spoken yet, of the true secret of Avon. Kings and their armies have trampled its banks from Naseby to Tewkesbury, performing great feats of war; castles and monasteries have risen over its waters; yet none of them has left a record so durable as are these grooves where the bargemen shifted their ropes in passing the bridge. The fighting reddened the river for a day; the building was reflected there for a century or two; but the slow toil of man has outlasted them both. And, looking westward over the homely landscape, we realized the truth that Nature, too, is most in earnest when least dramatic; that her most terrible power is seen neither in the whirlwind, nor in the earthquake, nor in the fire, but in the catkins budding on the hazel—the still, small voice that proves she is not dead, but sleeping lightly, and already dreaming of the spring.

Another striking passage in the book is Q's meditation as he stood before the tomb of Shakespeare in Stratford church:

It was easy now to forgive all that before had seemed unworthy in Stratford; easy, next morning, standing before Shakespeare's monument, while the sunshine, coloured by the eastern window, fell on one particular slab within the chancel rails, to live back for a moment to that April morning when a Shakespeare had passed from the earth, and earth 'must mourn therefor'; to follow his coffin on its short journey from the New Place, between the blossoming limes of the Church Walk, out of the sunlight into the lasting shadow, up the dim nave to this spot; and easy to divine, in the rugged epitaph so often quoted, the man's passionate dread lest his bones might be flung in time to the common charnel-house, the passionate longing to lie here always in this dusky corner, close to his friends and kin and the familiar voices that meant home—the talk of birds in the near elms, the chant of Holy Trinity choir, and, night and day, but a stone's-throw from his resting-place, the whisper of Avon running perpetually.

On returning from the Avon expedition Q settled in London with his wife. After living a few weeks in rooms at Oakley Street, Chelsea, and then a few weeks in rooms at Ladbroke Grove, they rented the house at Clareville Grove in which Q had lodged as a bachelor. Before the year was out Cassell's published his third novel, *The Splendid Spur, being Memoirs of the Adventures of Mr John Marvel, a Servant of his late Majesty King Charles I, in the years 1642–3, written by himself, edited in modern English by Q.*

The Splendid Spur is an adventure story in Stevensonian style: the very chapter-headings (like those in *Dead Man's Rock*) almost shout Stevenson's name at the reader. It goes with a swing from its beginning at Oxford to its ending in Cornwall and remained a favourite with the reading public over most of Q's other novels. The persistence and width of its appeal can be gauged from the fact that it was translated into Arabic more than fifty years later by one of Q's old pupils and had a big sale. It is worthy of note that *The Splendid Spur* has the earliest setting of all his novels, though a few of his short stories and his play, *The Regent*, stray into the sixteenth century. It is not surprising that he has no medieval settings, for (with Dante as almost the sole exception) he was not interested in the Middle Ages; but it is perhaps surprising that he wrote no novel with a Classical setting, particularly as he wove Classical themes very skilfully into some of his short stories.

In 1890 he gave up the house at Clareville Grove and, while his wife was in Cornwall, lodged for a time in rooms over a gun-smith's shop in St James's Street. He was now busy finishing his fourth novel, *The Blue Pavilions*, but most of his time was taken up with writing for Cassell's new weekly paper, *The Speaker*. He wrote for it from its first number, which appeared in January that year.

The founder and editor of *The Speaker* was Thomas Wemyss Reid, the biographer of Charlotte Brontë and W. E. Forster (and later of Lord Houghton and Gladstone), who had been general manager of Cassell's since 1887. His paper was to be concerned with politics, literature and the arts, and its politics were to be left-wing Liberalism. Looking round for a man of his own political persuasion to be assistant editor, Reid found him in Q, a convinced and life-long Liberal and a member of the left wing of the party despite his great love for tradition—or, as he himself would have put it, because of it. 'I have,' he said years later in one of his Cambridge lectures, 'a love of the past which, because it goes down to the roots, has sometimes been called Radicalism.'

The regular or semi-regular staff of *The Speaker* included J. M. Barrie, A. B. Walkley, George Moore, H. W. Massingham, L. F. Austin, Barry O'Brien, Richard Le Gallienne and Augustine

Birrell. Birrell was at the time Member of Parliament for West Fife and Q did not like him. 'That man takes himself much too seriously and nothing else seriously enough,' he once wrote to Wemyss Reid; and at another time he described Birrell as 'representing Fife as it ought to be represented—by wind'. Other more or less frequent contributors to the paper were Lord Acton, John Morley, James Bryce, J. A. Spender, Herbert Paul, Sidney Webb, James Payn, Henry James, Frederic Harrison and A. M. Fairbairn. In addition to these prose writers *The Speaker* had its poets, the chief being W. B. Yeats, John Davidson and William Watson. 'We met once a week for the lay-out of the paper', Q wrote, 'in a dingy room at the Craven Hotel. The paper was actually printed in La Belle Sauvage, where I used often to meet and lunch with Oscar Wilde (then in a magnificent coat of astrakhan, editing *The Woman's World*) and sometimes with George Moore. The both of these were good enough to treat me always as an intelligent listener—a game at which I can claim some ability to play.'

The chief rival of *The Speaker* was a right-wing Conservative paper, *The National Observer*, which was published next door. It was edited by W. E. Henley, who had Charles Whibley as his assistant editor. The staffs of the two papers were on very friendly terms and Barrie, though a Liberal, wrote for both, as did Yeats.

Before *The Speaker* began publication Q wrote to Wemyss Reid asking 'what banner of progress—literary or social' he was to hoist. 'I am even open,' he said, 'to attack (1) curates, (2) *Hymns Ancient and Modern*, on artistic grounds.' It was arranged that he should contribute literary *causeries* and reviews frequently and a short story once a week. He managed to satisfy these requirements and meanwhile to gain a reputation as a short-story writer. In September 1890 he wrote to Wemyss Reid:

Your readers must be pretty well tired of finding a short story by Q every week. So perhaps I had better do something else this time. Why has Barrie ceased work on this line? If there should be no prospect of a sketch from him *and* you particularly want one, send a wire and you shall have it....

I'm utterly dissatisfied with myself just now. Almost every day brings a request from some quarter or another for a short story. I feel I shall never write a big book and it worries me.

Many of his stories were written in the train between London and Fowey; others, as he tells us, 'under the stars over Plymouth Hoe in night-pacings through an interval thoughtfully provided for me by the Great Western, breaking trains on the way home'. A number of them—mostly reprinted from *The Speaker*—were published in book form in 1891 under the title, *Noughts and Crosses*. A further collection, called *I Saw Three Ships, and Other Winter's Tales*, appeared in the following year. These—it shows how hard he was working—were reprinted from periodicals other than *The Speaker*: from *The Illustrated London News, Yule Tide, Lloyd's Weekly News* and *The Weekly Dispatch*.

Noughts and Crosses, the first of his dozen volumes of short stories, was also the best of them. It put him at once into a very high place among English short-story writers. Several of its best stories, like so many that he wrote, are concerned with Cornish superstition and magic; such as the story of the mad Mayor of Gantick, 'who was wise for a long day and then died of it'; *Beside the Bee-hives*, in which a man rids himself of his wife by witchcraft; and *Psyche*, in which a mad engine-driver imagines that he sees his dead wife burnt to death a second time—this time in the form of a moth. (We find the same metempsychosis in Q's poem, *The White Moth*.) Another story in *Noughts and Crosses*—one of the most skilfully written of all his short stories—is *Old Aeson*. This was inspired by the birth of his first child, which took place at Fowey in October 1890. The child—a boy, christened Bevil Bryan—speedily became a great favourite with J. M. Barrie, whose letters contain many references to him under his pet names of 'Pippa' and 'Piper'.

Early in 1891 the family of three moved to 54 Bedford Gardens, Kensington. The house belonged to Alfred Parsons, who normally lived in it but was in Japan at the time and had lent it to Q for the period of his absence. Q's *Blue Pavilions*, published in the same year, was another adventure novel, its period being the reign of

William III. Cornwall does not come into the book but the sea runs all through it. Its object was, Q said, 'to infuse a sprinkling of the Shandean into an unhistorical-historical story which ran straight from a beginning, through a middle, to an end. Such a story had to deal with eccentrics, who are as natural (I conceive) in an English story as plums in a pudding.' The action quickens as the book goes on, particularly when the scene shifts to the Continent. Some of its incidents—life in the French galleys, for instance —and the ingenuous remarks of its young hero often remind the reader of Voltaire's *L'ingénu*; but the final note of the book is gentle and kind—very unlike Voltaire but very typical of Q.

Q was overworking badly and in the autumn of 1891 he had a serious breakdown. Early in 1892 he was suffering from insomnia and, as one of his old Oxford friends put it, was possessed by 'a nervous fear of crowds amounting even to shrinking from crossing the street'. He was induced to consult a specialist who, without knowing his history or his predilections, advised him to leave London if he could and live and work by the sea.

Q took the specialist's advice with great pleasure. 'Fleet Street,' he said long afterwards, 'was not my life. I made a great many wonderful friendships there. It was worth it for that alone, but I don't think I got anything else out of it—except an enhanced affection for home.' Having agreed to keep on working for *The Speaker* wherever he lived, he left London for Fowey shortly afterwards. His wife and child had been staying there since late in the previous year, so that he afterwards regarded 1891 as the year in which he left London for Fowey. When he joined his family early in 1892 they lived for six months in a small house that was afterwards converted into a boot shop. Before the summer was out they moved into a larger house, called The Haven, which Q rented at first. He soon came to love it and some years later bought it. It was his home until he died.

Q found peace as soon as he settled at Fowey. 'My calling', he wrote in an article which he contributed shortly afterwards to *The Idler*, 'ties me to no office stool, makes me no man's slave, compels me to no action that my soul condemns. It sets me free from town life, which I loathe, and allows me to breathe clean air, to exercise limbs as well as brain, to tread good turf and wake up every morning to the sound and smell of the sea and that wide prospect which to my eyes is the dearest on earth. All happiness must be purchased with a price, though people seldom recognize this: and part of the price is that, living thus, a man can never amass a fortune. But as it is extremely unlikely that I could have done this in any pursuit, I may claim to have the better of the bargain.'

CHAPTER IV

FOWEY: LATE NINETEENTH CENTURY
(1892-1900)

T HE estuary of the River Fowey forms a small but very attractive harbour with several picturesque creeks opening out of it and with green hills rising sharply from its waters on every side. Along its western shore, in little more than one long narrow street, stretches the ancient town of Fowey. In Kenneth Grahame's *Wind in the Willows* the Sea Rat describes it as 'the little grey sea town that clings along one steep side of the harbour. There through dark doorways you look down flights of stone steps, overhung by great pink tufts of valerian and ending in a patch of sparkling blue water. The little boats that lie tethered to the rings and stanchions of the old sea-wall are gaily painted; the salmon leap on the flood tide, schools of mackerel flash and play past quaysides and foreshores, and by the windows the great vessels glide, night and day, up to their moorings or forth to the open sea.'

The Sea Rat's 'great vessels' are not as big as they seemed to him; for the harbour, with its narrow entrance, will not take ships of more than 1500 tons. Those that come to Fowey deal mostly in china clay; but the harbour has lost none of its beauty through industrial development, because the wharves where the ships load their cargo are tucked out of sight above the town.

Except for its fine fourteenth-century church of St Finbar and the great Tudor house called Place (the home of the Treffrys) that stands over the town, everything in Fowey is on a miniature scale. 'It is but a toy town to look at,' J. M. Barrie wrote to the Dutch novelist Maarten Maartens, 'on a bay so small, hemmed in so picturesquely by cliffs and ruins that of a moonlight night it might pass for a scene in a theatre.' To the end of Q's life it had little more than 2500 inhabitants. One or two chain stores had by then, it is true, thrust their rubber-stamp shop-fronts among the local tradesmen, but they had at least had the decency not to rebuild on a scale that would have thrown everything else into disproportion.

The piece of land on which The Haven was built in 1877 is roughly triangular in shape. It is bounded on one side (220 feet) by the main street of Fowey. A path leading to the Polruan ferry forms a second boundary of about 100 feet and the house stands in the angle between this path and the street. The garden drops very steeply from the house to the water of the harbour, which forms the third boundary.

The second owner and occupier of The Haven—Q's immediate predecessor—was a naval lieutenant. He painted on the door of each room the name of some ship in which he had served and under the name he hung a water-colour painting of the ship from his own brush. The bathroom, not being a living room, had no name on its door; but, being a useful auxiliary, appropriately carried a painting of a ship's cutter. Q, with his inherited love for everything nautical, naturally allowed the names and the water-colours to stay where they were. The downstairs rooms were the *St Vincent* (which became Q's library and study), the *Royal Oak* (the drawing-room) and the *Victoria* (the dining-room). Those on the upper floor were the *Martin*, the *Iron Duke*, the *Britannia*, the *Arethusa*, the *Thalia*, the *Kestrel* and the *Dwarf*.

The house, Q wrote some years later,

is a plain one; indeed, very like the house a child draws on a slate, and therefore pleasing even externally to me, who prefer the classical to any Gothic style of architecture. Why so many strangers mistake it with its modest dimensions for a hotel, I cannot tell you. I found one in the pantry the other day searching for a brandy-and-soda; another rang the dining-room bell and dumbfoundered the maid by asking what we had for lunch; and a third (a lady) cried when I broke to her that I had no sitting-room to let. We make it a rule to send out a chair whenever some unknown invader walks into the garden and prepares to make a water-colour sketch of the view.

The Haven commands a charming view of the harbour and the open sea—a view that never lost its fascination for him. 'Of all views,' he wrote, 'I reckon that of a harbour the most fascinating and the most easeful, for it combines perpetual change with perpetual repose. It amuses like a panorama and soothes like an opiate, and when you have realized this you will understand why so many thousands of men around this island appear to spend all their time in watching tidal water.' The view from his windows was, he felt, more than ample compensation for the smallness of his garden; and not long after he acquired The Haven he wrote in a lady's album:

> I can't afford a mile of sward,
>   Parterres and peacocks gay;
> For velvet lawns and marble fauns
>   Mere authors cannot pay.
>
> And so I went and pitched my tent
>   Above a harbour fair,
> Where vessels picturesquely rigg'd
>   Obligingly repair.
>
> The harbour is not mine at all:
>   I make it so—What odds?
> And gulls unwitting on my wall
>   Serve me for garden-gods.
>
> By ships that ride below kaleid-
>   oscopically changed,
> Unto my mind each day I find
>   My garden rearranged.
>
> These, madam, are my daffodils,
>   My pinks, my hollyhocks,
> My herds upon a hundred hills,
>   My phloxes and my flocks.
>
> And when some day you deign to pay
>   The call that's overdue,
> I'll wave a landlord's easy hand
>   And say, 'Admire *my* view!'

The Haven, Fowey
above from the harbour
below from the garden

Residence at The Haven had an excellent effect on his health, though he did not recover fully until about the end of 1893. In November 1892 he wrote to Wemyss Reid:

I wish I could come up and see you about the *Speaker* and other exciting matters: but it would take me three days on the road up in my present state. The nerves are much better and I can do a little work again: but I still get floored after more than an hour or two in the train. To begin with, I couldn't stand five minutes of it, and I want to get thoroughly out of this mess before running the risk of breaking down the improvement of these last six months.

In December he wrote:

in these last three weeks I seem (though I say it with bated breath) to have made more headway than in the previous six months, and hope I shall be fit to do my share of the work respectably;

and in August 1893 he wrote:

I am gradually coming to feel myself a sound man and also to realize that eighteen months have slipped away and left me in the rear of all my contemporaries—which isn't a pleasant reflection. But I really have notions and mean to do something in the next twelve months, with luck.

He certainly carried out his determination to 'do something'. During the first seven years after he settled at Fowey he not only contributed regularly to *The Speaker* but also wrote or edited more than a dozen books.

The first of these was a collection of short stories, mostly reprinted from *The Speaker* and concerned almost entirely with Cornish life. One day about Easter 1893, when he was pacing the sands at St Ives, wondering what to call the book, a title suddenly struck him—*The Delectable Duchy*. This happy invention made an immediate hit with the public and soon came into general use as a name for Cornwall. His volume of light verse, called *Green Bays*, which came out in the same year, consisted mainly of parodies reprinted from *The Oxford Magazine*. A collection of his more serious verse, entitled *Poems and Ballads*, followed three years later. It opened with a poem *Upon New Year's Eve*, which exemplifies

the delight that Q always took in the simplicities of country life
and contains a charming tribute to his wife:

> Now winds of winter glue
>   Their tears upon the thorn,
> And earth has voices few,
>   And those forlorn.
>
> And 'tis our solemn night
>   When maidens sand the porch,
> And play at Jack's Alight
>   With burning torch,
>
> Or cards, or Kiss i' the Ring—
>   While ashen faggots blaze,
> And late wassailers sing
>   In miry ways.
>
> Then, dear my wife, be blithe
>   To bid the New Year hail,
> And welcome—plough, drill, scythe,
>   And jolly flail.
>
> For though the snows he'll shake
>   Of winter from his head,
> To settle, flake by flake,
>   On ours instead;
>
> Yet we be wreathèd green
>   Beyond his blight or chill,
> Who kissed at seventeen,
>   And worship still.
>
> We know not what he'll bring:
>   But this we know to-night—
> He doth prepare the Spring
>   For our delight.
>
> With birds he'll comfort us,
>   With blossoms, balms, and bees,
> With brooks, and odorous
>   Wild breath o' the breeze.

> Come then, O festal prime!
>   With sweets thy bosom fill,
> And dance it, dripping thyme,
>   On Lantick hill.
>
> West wind, awake! and comb
>   Our garden, blade from blade—
> We, in our little home,
>   Sit unafraid.

This poem had already appeared in 1895 in the prologue to a third collection of his stories, which he called *Wandering Heath*. It contained some stories that had appeared in *The Speaker*, but most of them were from other periodicals. In the same year he published his first anthology of English verse, entitled *The Golden Pomp, a Procession of English Lyrics from Surrey to Shirley*, which he dedicated to A. J. Butler. Its compilation had occupied him during his convalescence from illness a few years before. 'What a noble title!' Richard Le Gallienne wrote to Q: 'It was a particularly happy hour when you thought of it. The mere look of it on the back of the book suggests banners and bugles and the joyous tread of armed men.'

The following year saw the publication of his first critical work, *Adventures in Criticism*—a reprint, with a few alterations, of a number of his causeries contributed to *The Speaker* between the beginning of 1891 and the end of 1895. One of them is a gallant defence of Laurence Sterne against the diatribes of Thackeray. It remarks that even Charles Whibley, who had been a member of Sterne's old college at Cambridge and had recently written about him, could not 'get quit of the bad tradition of patronizing Sterne'. Another article in the book records Q's feelings on first hearing of the death of Robert Louis Stevenson: 'Put away books and paper and pen. Stevenson is dead. Stevenson is dead, and now there is nobody left to write for.'

In view of Q's devotion to Stevenson and the manifest ease with which he wrote in his style, it was not surprising that Sidney Colvin, Stevenson's literary executor, invited him to complete the novel, *St Ives*, which Stevenson left unfinished when he died.

Q himself was amazed at the invitation but accepted it and the completed book was published in 1898. Writing thirty years later, he said:

> The invitation flattered a young man too far to be declined. Actually, it was not, to any reader soaked in Stevenson, so very difficult—save that the few notes left made the finish of the story almost impossible. Anyone who knows anything about the writing of a story will understand that that (barring the restraint imposed by certain notes indicating the way to its conclusion—these almost absurd as they stood, but religiously observed) was as easy as to conclude the other unfinished book, *Weir of Hermiston*, had been impossible.

Q's share in *St Ives* is only slightly less than a quarter of the whole. It has been highly praised and rightly so, for anyone who did not know would find great difficulty in detecting where the one author ended his work and the other began. Those who criticize Q's part of the book on the ground that its incidents are absurd are obviously unaware that they are criticizing Stevenson rather than Q.

Apart from his short stories, Q's own fiction had hitherto been compounded predominantly of two elements—adventure and humour. In *Ia*, published in 1896, he turned aside from both of these to the study of character. *Ia* proved the truth of Henry Newbolt's prophecy (made several years after the event) that Q 'would never settle down into the comfortable position of a writer of Stevensonian tales for the young of all ages'. It is a brief but moving story, most delicately and beautifully told, of a poor Cornish fisher-girl's love and devotion for a man of superior station who is unworthy of her and whom in the end she refuses to marry, though she still loves him. One of the other characters in the book—the local doctor, who does a great work during a serious epidemic in the poverty-stricken village of Ardevora—is evidently drawn from Q's father. The doctor in the novel, who teaches the quick-witted Ia to nurse, resembles Thomas Couch in being, as Q said of his father, 'a sceptic on many points of traditional medicine' and in possessing 'a strong belief in the efficacy of nursing'.

Though *Ia* is one of Q's best novels it did not have a good sale—perhaps because it is only about half the usual length of a novel. Barrie, to whom it was dedicated, admired it and wrote to Q at the end of 1896: 'I should feel very miserable if I thought you were getting despondent about your books because they have not a large sale. Go back to the *Dead Man's Rock* business and you will at once be in the running with the most popular men of the day. But go on doing your best and you have a reward which is the only real reward and as it seems to me the only thing that makes this calling of letters a manly one.'

Q's next novel, *The Ship of Stars*, published three years later, is another study of character and contains a good deal of auto-biography. He intended it, he wrote thirty years afterwards, 'to be a sort of diploma-piece attesting the piety of a son of Oxford, who had perforce broken away from her'. The hero of the book, Taffy Raymond, is born, like Q, at Bodmin. Q's vivid memories of his own childhood provide a number of incidents in Taffy's childhood—such as his interest in the visits of the county militia to Bodmin, his lying awake at night and listening to their bugles and his first visit to a theatre at Plymouth. Like Q, Taffy becomes an undergraduate at Oxford and while he is there his father dies. This stops his University career, as the death of Q's father nearly stopped his. Thereafter he makes his way by his own efforts, as Q did. Towards the end of the book we get a statement of the hero's philosophy of life, which was Q's also:

In later days Taffy maintained not only that every man must try to stand alone, but that he ought to try the harder because of its impossibility; for in fact it was impossible to escape from men's helpfulness. And though his work was done in lonely places where in the end fame came out to seek him, he remained the same boy who, waking in the dark, had heard the bugles speaking comfort.

Here Q describes himself better than he knew, particularly in the last sentence; for, more than most men, he remained fundamentally unchanged throughout life and still had the heart of a boy when he died at the age of eighty. *The Ship of Stars* is, as Sidney Colvin put it, 'remarkably fresh and vivid, well felt and well written'. It was Q's best novel, partly because of its excellent characterization and partly because it contained so much of its author's personality.

In the same year he published his *Historical Tales from Shakespeare*, which aimed at doing for the historical plays what Charles and Mary Lamb had done for the tragedies and comedies. The book was dedicated 'To Algernon Charles Swinburne, who with the nearest claim among living men to approach Shakespeare confidently has with the best right set them the example of reverent and humble study.' Swinburne, in accepting the dedication, wrote to Q as follows:

> The Pines,
> Putney Hill.
> 5 September 1899

Dear Sir,

No other compliment could have given me so much pleasure as your proposal to dedicate your *Historical Tales from Shakespeare* to me. It is not only a great honour, it is a great pleasure to be told that my criticism or study of the greatest man that ever lived had been, as you are good enough to say, of service to a student such as you.

I think you have most happily eluded the difficulty about the parentage of the hero of Faulconbridge—a friend of mine ever since I was seven years old, when I did not in the least trouble myself about the meaning of the prefix 'Bastard'. Of course it was dear good old Bowdler's edition in which I was permitted to make acquaintance with him and his Divine creator. As to Joan of Arc—of course you could not and would not 'copy into a book designed for young readers' the shameful caricature and libel for which I am almost absolutely certain that Shakespeare is no more responsible than you or I.... And as you go in for historical accuracy—quite rightly, need I say? in my opinion— I certainly think you ought not to leave your young readers under the false impression that Joan the Maid was murdered by the English.... I think you are very hard on the Plantagenets whom Tennyson thought 'England's mightiest kings'—the best of them, that is. But you have managed the Wars of the Roses—a severe test—most admirably.

> Yours very gratefully,
>
> A. C. SWINBURNE.

He added a typical postscript which was probably less appreciated by its recipient than its writer confidently expected:

I think you may like to know that the author of *Aylwin* is a great admirer of *The Silver* (sic) *Spur*.

During these early years at Fowey, when Q's time was so fully occupied with his weekly articles for *The Speaker* and his numerous other writings, he nevertheless managed to keep in touch with old friends and to make new ones. William Robertson Nicoll spent a week with him in 1892; and Barrie, who now and then reproached Q as 'a low ruffian' for not answering his letters, stayed in rooms at Fowey in the same year and spent much of his time at The Haven. In 1893 Q wrote to Wemyss Reid: 'I wish to heaven you would catch Barrie, pack him in a box and send him down here in a violently oscillating steamer that he may cast up all the devils within him and arrive here clean and ready for the talk I want to shovel into him.' In July 1894 Barrie wrote to Q from London to announce his engagement to Mary Ansell:

Yes, it is all true, though it was in the papers, and I am just recovering from the pleasure of having a letter on the subject—yours—which is not comic. Even so long ago as when I was going to you in Bedford Gardens I was beginning to hope that this would come about, and I am not in a position to deny, as the *Speaker* would say, that the obvious happiness of you two seemed to me a most enviable thing.

In the autumn Barrie brought his wife to Fowey. They stayed in rooms in the town, as he had done in 1892, but spent many hours at The Haven, where Barrie derived great pleasure from playing with Bevil, now four years old. 'He is my favourite boy in the wide wide world,' he wrote afterwards to Q.

Q's new correspondents about this time included Maarten Maartens, whom he met in later years and admired greatly, and James Dryden Hosken, a poor Cornish poet for whose *Verses by the Way* he wrote an Introduction. This was the first of a long line of Introductions that he generously wrote for other men's books in order to help struggling authors or good causes. The same local patriotism that made him particularly interested in Hosken

33

prompted him to found and edit *The Cornish Magazine* in 1898; but it was badly supported and came to an end in the following year after eleven monthly issues.

It was in the spring of 1899 that Q first met Kenneth Grahame, who was staying at the Fowey Hotel convalescing after a very severe attack of pneumonia. The two became friends at once and were friends for life. Grahame and his fiancée liked Fowey so much that they decided to get married there that summer. During the three Sundays on which their banns were called in Fowey Church the bridegroom stayed at The Haven. A few days before the wedding the bride and her relations came and stayed at the Fowey Hotel, as did also the best man—Anthony Hope Hawkins, the novelist, who was Grahame's cousin. Being fond of practical jokes he hired a hurdy-gurdy man to grind his organ outside The Haven on the wedding morning and wake the household at an early hour. After the wedding, Mr and Mrs Grahame came back to Fowey for the latter part of their honeymoon. They spent much of it sailing with Q in his yacht, the *Vida*, or rowing round the harbour with him in his red boat, the *Picotee*, or in their own boat, the *Richard and Emily*.

Boats, oars and sails provided Q's chief relaxation throughout life, from his school-days onwards. He was an early member of the Fowey Yacht Club and very soon became prominent in it. He enjoyed sailing, but he got quite as much enjoyment out of the social side of the club or out of pulling round the harbour and its creeks in a rowing boat, exploring, meditating, fishing, or calling on friends. He equally enjoyed teaching the boys of Fowey Grammar School the art of racing with the oar.

Some years after he settled at Fowey he wrote to Maarten Maartens: 'I live almost a hermit's life down here, writing and sailing my boat', but he was in fact doing far more than that. He was already taking a part in public affairs which, even if it was as yet mostly unofficial, was nevertheless considerable. Always willing to help a good cause, he would at any time put his pen at the disposal of local charities and write letters to the papers on their behalf, or compose short stories or verses for sale at bazaars. Once

he produced a whole booklet of verse for the local hospital—
A Fowey Garland, with its pleasant nonsense-verses:

> O the harbour of Fowey
>   Is a beautiful spot,
> And it's there I enjowey
>   To sail in a yot;
> Or to race in a yacht
>   Round a mark or a buoy—
> Such a beautiful spacht
>   Is the harbour of Fuoy!...

In 1897 he helped to organize the local celebration of Queen
Victoria's Diamond Jubilee. The celebration took place on 22 June
and Q's enthusiasm was such that he rose at four o'clock in the
morning to supervise the arrangements for the day. He revelled in
observances of the kind and this was but the first of a number of
occasions on which he helped Fowey to take its full share in national
rejoicings. He wrote to Sidney Colvin afterwards:

> We performed great feats here on Jubilee Day. I worked the people
> up and we lined the streets with trees from end to end and put up
> arches and criss-crossed all between with lanterns and bunting until
> I had a mile of green bazaar. And we fed 1850 handsomely by the
> water-side—let alone 350 sailors, British and foreign, Swedes, Russians,
> Italians, infidels and hereticks—and marched and countermarched by
> hundreds in fancy dress under the lanterns and then danced till the
> gunpowder ran out of the heels of our boots.
>
> The local band under our windows roused us out at 7 a.m. and we
> crept to bed at 3 a.m. In short, sir, the place went off its head—*and
> we hadn't a man drunk*: a few merry but not what-you-may-call-
> drunk. The town has been shaking hands upon it ever since.

Not long after the Diamond Jubilee, however, Q's growing
popularity at Fowey received a temporary check with many of the
local people owing to his attitude towards the South African War
of 1899–1902. The nation as a whole was carried away by war-
fever. Q, on the other hand, not only believed that the war was
wrong, but also stated his opinion openly. Further, when the
local Member of Parliament, Leonard Courtney, who shared his

opinions about the war, asked him to take the chair at an anti-war meeting to be held at Liskeard, he readily accepted the invitation. It was a risky thing to do, because the principal speaker was to be David Lloyd George, who at the time was regarded as a firebrand and was loathed by the imperialists for his vehement pro-Boer speeches in various parts of the country. Q must have had some very uncomfortable moments when, during his opening speech, a note was passed up to him from someone in the audience warning him that a man was present with a revolver, with which he intended to shoot Lloyd George. The audience allowed Q to finish his speech and then stormed the platform and brought the meeting to an end, though the threat to shoot Lloyd George was not carried out.

The war made Maarten Maartens very unhappy, for he loved England but (being a Dutchman) could not help sympathizing strongly with the Boers. Q wrote to him to cheer him up and said:

The war has made me unhappy too. On many points we should not agree: for Kruger and his party seem to me to have behaved in a way that made it very hard for England to use patience. At the same time I have always believed that by patience the war might have been averted, and still believe that force is no final remedy for South Africa—and have been called vile names and even assaulted on a platform for saying so: which, if we met, might help you to overlook the points on which we should probably differ.

I see no hope against this accursed militarism through which we are all moving towards slavery until those who, in all nations, believe in spiritual things organize themselves to make this belief felt. The Church tried it once, and the old Papal policy at the time of the Crusades was one of the finest things in history—there was never a nobler idea than that of erecting throughout Europe an Empire of intellect and conscience which should dictate to princes and bind all nations in faith and peace. But I doubt if any Church will rise to such an idea again: and only a miracle could produce an instrument so splendidly efficient as a priesthood without the corruption which a priesthood carries in itself.

But I don't think this hopelessness lessens the obligation to shout in the wilderness—scattered and inefficient as we seem.

By this time, Q's connection with *The Speaker* had ended. In June 1899 he received a letter from Wemyss Reid telling him that he was giving up the editorship of the paper, which was to have a change of proprietor as well as of editor on 1 October. The letter continued:

My successors are some clever young Oxonians (Hirst, Hammond, Belloc, etc.) who are thirsting for distinction in journalism and who will doubtless make the *Speaker* a much more brilliant paper than it has ever been under my humdrum charge. I am forced by my agreement with the new proprietors formally to terminate all existing arrangements as from October 1st. I do this in your case with particular pain.

I shall never forget our early days of storm and stress on the *Speaker* and the zealous and invaluable help you then gave me. I have wished a thousand times that your health would have permitted you to remain in London by my side. Many things might then have been different.

Q replied:

My dear Reid,

Your letter came this evening, and I am writing at once: not because I know what to say—for I don't.

But I needn't try to say how sorry I am. You must know. All friendliness apart, if it were only that you gave me with the *Speaker* my first chance and have let me go on under you for something like ten years, your letter would mean the end of a great deal for me. But my start with it opened the happiest time of my life. And does it occur to you that in all the time you've never spoken or sent me an angry word? I must remember these things: and your letter means the end of more than I care to think about.

It *has* been a good paper. It has always been my pride to have written in the first number. We shall see what these new men will make of it: but I'll swear they'll never make us ashamed of the old days and efforts. And if some of us talked lightly, as a habit, you never doubted (I hope) that we were loyal and proud in our hearts of the paper and its editor.

You mustn't bother about me. I find that, while one can work, work tumbles in: but I hope Mann and Perris will not get 'left'. What a crew of us you have had to command, first and last! Upon my word we ought to get ourselves photographed—Barrie and Birrell, Mann, Perris, Austin, O'Brien, Barry Pain, A. B. W. and Mrs Reilly: with Fairbairn and Bryce invoking a blessing on either wing and yourself in the act of erasing one of poor F.'s paragraphs. It *has* been a thundering good paper. It has always fought honourably and scrupulously, too: though these ten years have meant the most trying battle Liberalism has had to fight for the century. When the time comes for cheering I hope the *Speaker* and your editing of it will be remembered. But we shall remember, anyhow: and it won't matter if we *do* mix it up with memories of your kindness to us.

Ever yours,

A. T. QUILLER-COUCH.

Although Q finished writing for *The Speaker* in 1899 he kept on taking it. In 1907 it changed its name to *The Nation* and in 1931 was incorporated in *The New Statesman*. He still kept on taking it but was often very irritated with its contents. It is true that *The Statesman* stood further to the political Left than *The Speaker* had done, yet it was its manner rather than its politics that annoyed him. He often exclaimed with great vehemence: 'I will *not* take this paper any longer. I will see my newsagent about it to-morrow.' His friends, knowing him to be a man of great loyalties, took no notice of what he said: they knew that he would never bring himself to cancel his order for the descendant of *The Speaker*. He was still taking it when he died.

Q had remarked in his letter to Wemyss Reid: 'Work tumbles in.' It was certainly tumbling in at the time and continued to do so. He was preparing for the press yet another volume of his short stories, mostly concerned with phantoms and mysteries— *Old Fires and Profitable Ghosts*, one of the most fascinating of all his books. Above all, he was reading omnivorously for the great anthology of English verse which Charles Cannan (by this time secretary to the Clarendon Press) had asked him to compile. His preparatory reading stretched from the thirteenth century to the end of the nineteenth and embraced any country 'wheresoever the Muse has followed the tongue which among living tongues she most delights to honour'. The result of his labours, *The Oxford*

Book of English Verse, was published in 1900. It was received rather coldly at first, but after a year or two came rapidly into favour and won recognition as the finest anthology of English verse that had ever been published. In 1912 *The Oxford Magazine* jocularly remarked that 'no civilized person in Great Britain, the Dominions or the United States is married or given in marriage' without being presented with one or more copies of the *Oxford Book*. By 1939 it had been reprinted twenty times and nearly half a million copies had been sold.

CHAPTER V

FOWEY: EARLY TWENTIETH CENTURY
(1901–12)

DURING the twelve years that elapsed between the publication of *The Oxford Book of English Verse* and his return to an academical life, Q's literary output was remarkable in its variety and astonishing in its extent. It included a volume of poems, a volume of essays, three anthologies (among them *The Oxford Book of Ballads* and *The Oxford Book of Victorian Verse*), several children's books (either written or edited by him), forty or more brief selections from various English writers with Introductions, and twenty volumes of fiction, among which were no fewer than thirteen novels. Of all the thirteen, not one is dull, not one can be called poor, and no two are alike. They possess, indeed, a remarkable variety of setting, of treatment, of incident and of character.

Three of the thirteen are pre-eminently studies of female character. In *The Westcotes*, which is no longer than *Ia*, Q handles with great delicacy, even with reverence, a theme that very few writers would take the trouble to handle at all, unless it were to poke fun—the love of an unattractive, middle-aged spinster for a man much younger than herself. In *Hetty Wesley*, which the public subsequently liked more than any of his other novels, authentic documents are interspersed with invented narrative to tell the story of his heroine's unhappy life and the severity with which she was treated by her father, the Reverend Samuel Wesley, and her brothers John and Charles. When the Methodist press criticized the book severely, on the ground that it gave an unfair picture of the Wesley family, Q retorted that it was the book of his that he could regard with most satisfaction, 'and certainly with a satisfaction impossible to one who doubted its essential truth'. The controversy quietened down in time; and when he died a writer in the leading Methodist weekly generously admitted that 'Q's purpose was good, and a later generation, less touchy, can the more appreciate what the writer was anxious to say'. Q wrote in defence of a woman again in *Lady Good-for-Nothing*, once more choosing the eighteenth century but this time laying his scene for the most part in Massachusetts and for the rest at Lisbon during the great earthquake of 1755.

In *Fort Amity* he again laid his scene in North America, this time during the Seven Years' War. With such a setting one might expect from Q a pure adventure story; but, as Sir Henry Newbolt (to whom the book is dedicated) says in his *Later Life and Letters*, *Fort Amity* is rather a study of 'the effect of war upon the nerves and character of a young officer in a perplexing and desperate campaign. It is perhaps the earliest case on record—certainly the first described sympathetically in fiction—of the malady or injury of war-misery for which our generation invented the name shell-shock.'

Q returned to the pure adventure story in *Harry Revel*, which opens at Plymouth in 1813 and ends at Ciudad Rodrigo; also in *True Tilda*, in which two precocious children make their way through Q's *Warwickshire Avon* country to the sea. He used some of the characters from *Harry Revel* again in *Poison Island*—a less thoroughly Stevensonian book than its title would lead one to expect. Intended to be a compound of Stevenson and Dickens it is, rather, Stevenson with a dash of Cervantes.

The Cervantes strain is very strong indeed in *Sir John Constantine* (1906), which was Q's favourite among all his novels. It relates the adventures of a Cornish knight in Corsica during the eighteenth century but is something much more than a story of adventure: it is a twentieth-century version of *Don Quixote*—a book that haunted Q most of his life. He wrote it after long familiarity with Cervantes and after reading some such work as Percy Fitzgerald's biography of the German adventurer, Theodore von Neuhof, who was nominally King of Corsica for a time during the eighteenth century. *Sir John Constantine* is certainly one of the best of Q's novels and contains much of his personality.

We find the Cervantes element again, though less strong, in *The*

Mayor of Troy, published in the same year as *Sir John Constantine*. One of the best known of all Q's works, it tells how the pompous and apparently indispensable Mayor is taken prisoner by the French during the Napoleonic wars. On returning from captivity several years later he finds that he was not indispensable after all and goes away again in sorrow. When Q consulted Barrie about the possibility of converting the book into a play Barrie replied: 'I think there is no doubt of the *idea* of *The Mayor of Troy* being right for stage treatment', but suggested some alterations. As he had in his notes, he said, 'an idea not dissimilar', he proposed that they should write the play jointly and publish it under an assumed name. This project lay dormant for a time. When it was revived five years later Barrie wrote to Q: 'I should be very glad to help in any sort of way with that play; there is no doubt about its being a fine subject, but the difficulty is that it seems to lead to a grim end and rather a queer view of life altogether. I have often thought of it in three acts and see the first two all right. The third seems to amount to this: no one should come back, however much he was loved.' In the end Q wrote his play alone and Barrie wrote his *Mary Rose* on the theme that 'no one should come back, however much he was loved'. His was a serious treatment of a theme which Q had all along treated humorously and extravagantly. In his preface to a later edition of *The Mayor of Troy* Q said:

Did my pen in telling of Troy eschew extravagance, the poor thing would run false to truth and nature. For this dearest of small cities lives, breathes and runs its daily self-respecting life in extravaganza, so confounding the categories of Tragedy and Comedy that Aristotle himself would have to abandon definition and fall back here on his saving clause that 'we must not at all costs keep to the received legends';

and in a letter to a friend he said:

Yes. *The Mayor* ends its comedy upon rather a sad note. I even plead guilty of intending it, and, *si parva licet*—would quote you, by way of warrant, no less a masterpiece than *Don Quixote*. Where will you find sadder writing than the chapter in which the Don rides home to his native village?

In fact I am prepared to argue with you that the distinction between tragedy and comedy is a highly artificial and arbitrary one. But of course if the telling of the story pulled you up with a sudden change of style my writing was at fault—and I dare say it was.

Q made 'this dearest of small cities' the scene of two more of his novels—*Shining Ferry* and *Hocken and Hunken*, both of which have settings of his own time. *Shining Ferry* reflects Q's educational work in the county—particularly in its description of the supplanting of the old-fashioned dame schools by the new rate-supported elementary schools. *Hocken and Hunken*, which is pure comedy, contains a close study of one of Q's chief yearly delights —the regatta at 'Troy'.

In *Major Vigoureux*, published in 1907, the scene moves from Fowey to another part of Cornwall—the Scilly Isles—and the heroine utters those 'Land for the People' sentiments that formed the slogan of Q's political party at the time when the book was being written. When she addresses the proprietor of the islands she speaks not only for those who had in fact been ejected from one of the smaller of the Scillies some years before, but also for Q, with his passionate love of the soil—the Q who was descended from generations of yeomen and seafarers, the Radical Q who was working ardently in the Liberal cause. 'You defend', she says, 'an instinct of selfishness that takes about five minutes to pass into a principle with any man who buys land. You maintain the landlord's right to ordain the lives on your estate, and command them to be as you think best; nor does it seem to you to affect your claim for power that we understood and drew our nurture from the islands before you ever came to hear of them.' 'Radicalism, ma'am!' 'Yes, sir. It is for the roots I plead, against your claim that the surface gives all.'

Q's political and philosophical creed is extensively set out in his novel, *Brother Copas*, published in 1911. The scene is laid at 'St Hospital, Merchester', about 1908–9; that is to say, at the ancient almshouses known as the Hospital of St Cross, Winchester —the original of Trollope's 'Hiram's Hospital'—which Q had probably visited more than once between 1904 and 1909, when his son was at school at Winchester. 'In *Sir John Constantine*', he says in his preface, 'I expressed (perhaps extravagantly) my faith in my fellows and in their capacity to treat life as a noble sport. In *Brother Copas* I try to express something of that correlative scorn which must come sooner or later to every man who puts his faith into practice. I hold the faith still; but that

> He who would love his fellow men
> Must not expect too much of them

is good counsel if bad rhyme. I can only hope that both the faith and scorn are sound at the core.' The book describes the lives of the pensioners at St'Hospital, the gossip and scandal-mongering among them and their wives, and the dissatisfaction of some of them with the ecclesiastical practices of the chaplain. It ends, as any picture of contemporary English life in the latter part of Edward VII's reign might well end, with a local pageant, evidently drawn from the Winchester pageant of 1908. Its chief interest, however, is to be found in the opinions of Brother Copas, which are those of the author himself. He has the same patriotism as Q, the same recognition of the national failings, the same Liberalism, the same dislike of German critics of English literature, the same conviction that *Beowulf* is 'no rugged national epic at all, but a blown-out bag of bookishness'. He even studies the *Pervigilium Veneris*, the text of which Q was preparing for the press at the time, and translates part of it into the English version that Q published next year in his *Vigil of Venus and Other Poems*. Taken as a whole, *Brother Copas* by no means lives down to the cynicism that anyone who did not know Q would expect from it after reading the preface. His natural goodness of heart forced him to write a book that reminds one of Mr Edwards's remark to Dr Johnson: 'I have tried in my time to be a philosopher; but, I don't know how, cheerfulness was always breaking in'.

Q's preoccupation with his novels and numerous other literary works did not prevent him from taking part—and an ever increasing part—in public affairs in Cornwall as a whole and at Fowey in particular. As at the Diamond Jubilee of 1897, so at the

E.  R.

Coronation of King Edward VII.

FOWEY

Programme of Festivities, June 26th, 1902.

8 a.m.	The Festivities of the day will be ushered in by the **RINGING of the CHURCH BELLS**
9 a.m.	The Children will assemble outside the Railway Station for the **DISTRIBUTION of MEDALS** By Mrs. QUILLER-COUCH, and Mrs. HAYTON, (Medals presented by C. A. HANSON, Esq.,) after which
9.30 a.m.	A PROCESSION Of the Royal Naval Reserve, The Fowey Artillery Volunteers, Free Masons, Foresters, Rechabites, School Children and Inhabitants generally, headed by the VOLUNTEER BAND, (by permission of Capt. Carnall), will march by way of the Principal Streets to the Church Yard, to witness the **PLANTING OF** # Coronation Trees By Mrs. TREFFRY, and Mrs. PURCELL. This Ceremony will be accompanied by Song.
10.30 a.m.	THE # Coronation Service Will follow in the Parish Church: after which the Volunteers will parade and march to the Town Quay and there fire **"A FEU DE JOIE"**
1.30 p.m.	ATHLETIC SPORTS (For which Prizes will be offered) will be held **IN THE GRAMMAR SCHOOL FIELD.** See Bills.
4 p.m.	# A Children's Tea (At which each Child will receive a MUG) Will be provided AROUND THE TOWN QUAY, to be followed by
5 p.m.	# A PUBLIC TEA For all Adult Inhabitants of Fowey, on presentation of Invitation Cards issued by the Committee.
9 p.m.	A GRAND # Procession of Lanterns Headed by the VOLUNTEER BAND will start from the RAILWAY STATION, and parade the Town. Inhabitants are requested to assemble with their Lanterns, in FANCY DRESS, at 8-30 p.m. The Committee will feel obliged if as many as possible will illuminate their houses in time for the Procession, and if in doing so they will take all possible precautions.
10 p.m.	**Illumination of the Harbour** WITH COLOURED LIGHTS.
10.30 p.m.	**A FANCY DRESS BALL** Will be held in the Town Hall and Working Men's Institute. Open to all over 16 years of age. Tickets 1/- (see bills).

GOD SAVE THE KING.

E. J. ROSCORLA, Printer and Stationer, FOWEY.

Programme of Coronation Festivities at Fowey in 1902
(The coronation had to be postponed until 9 August, owing to the King's illness)

Coronation of King Edward VII in 1902 he took a large share in arranging the local rejoicings. An official poster that has survived from the latter year repeats a similar document of 1897 almost word for word and gives a good idea of the festivities at Fowey. One can see Q's hand behind it all, although he was obviously not responsible for the entire wording of the poster, with its unintentional suggestion that the Coronation itself was to take place in Fowey parish church.

The natives of small country towns in England are notoriously slow to appreciate the virtues of those who, having been born elsewhere, come to live amongst them; and Fowey, by allowing Q to play a big part in the celebrations of 1897 and 1902, had shown that it had taken him to its heart. The standing that he had acquired locally (in spite of his attitude towards the Boer War) is well expressed in a letter written in 1904 by Maarten Maartens during his first visit to Fowey, after corresponding with Q for ten years. Writing to Mrs Edmund Gosse on Easter Day, he said:

This is quite an exquisite place; do you know it? Quiller-Couch and his home and his surroundings and family quite ideal. I have never heard you speak of them. King of Fowey in a quiet way—and such a kingdom!—with a delightful little Yacht Club next door for the civilized world to turn up in, handy, at tea time. What good fortune to be born to! The day has been supremely enjoyable—an exquisite old church in the morning: on the bay and river all the afternoon, to a delightful highly cultivated friend just across the water, with two rooms full of pictures, several first rate, especially the water-colours.

Of Q's numerous other visitors, Barrie was not one. He often talked of revisiting Fowey but, becoming more and more absorbed in his literary career, never did so. He nevertheless retained his affection for Q and met him occasionally elsewhere. In 1906 he wrote to Q: 'I think it's truth that you are what I miss mostly in London. It would have made a big difference to me if you had been here all these years.' In 1909 he wrote: 'I miss you much and always. On the whole I've cared for you more than any other of our calling'; and in 1903: 'I think it is the truth to say that in these 40 years I have met no man that has meant as much to me'. When

Q's daughter was born—Foy Felicia, the second and last child of the marriage—Barrie stood godfather to her. He retained his interest in Bevil and in 1905 went with Q to pay him a visit at Winchester College. 'The Boy!' he wrote to Q in 1909; 'to think he is leaving Winchester instead of putting on his pinafore! To-morrow he will be leaving Oxford.'

Q found time for many activities besides writing for his living, entertaining and yachting. He began to be appointed to public offices about the beginning of the century; and within a few years he was a prominent figure in Cornish local government—vice-chairman of the County Education Committee, a county alderman, a justice of the peace, chairman of the Commissioners of Fowey Harbour, chairman of the Sub-commissioners of Pilotage for the Fowey District, and president of the Fowey Mercantile Association, as well as being a leader in the political affairs of his constituency.

He took his magisterial duties, as he took all his duties, very seriously and acquired the reputation of being an impartial administrator of justice with a bias towards leniency. His experiences on the bench are reflected in some of his short stories, in which he gives humorous descriptions of petty sessional courts held under the chairmanship of an imaginary Sir Felix Felix-Williams, the squire of Kirris-vean. Anyone unacquainted with Cornwall might be pardoned for thinking that the names of Q's magisterial district and its constituent parishes are also imaginary. They form a poem in themselves:

THE HUNDRED OF POWDER
Tywardreath, Luxulyan, Lanlivery,
Saint Sampson's, Lostwithiel, Fowey.

Q's work for Cornish education, which was to be one of the chief interests of his life, began in 1904, when he was co-opted to membership of the County Education Committee in succession to Thomas King, a non-resident Fellow of Jesus College, Cambridge, who had recently died. He remained a member of the committee for thirty years and was either vice-chairman or chairman for all but the first three years. 'I like recreation as much as most men', he wrote in *From a Cornish Window*, 'and have grown to find it in the dull but deeply absorbing business of sitting on education committees'. It is true that he came to love the work: that he did so, and that he served so long, is great testimony to his self-discipline and sense of duty, for he was a man who found attendance at business meetings a strain all through life.

When he joined the committee it had existed only a few months. It had come into being in September 1903 under the provisions of the Balfour Education Act of 1902, which was a landmark in the history of English education. The Act gave wide powers over both elementary and secondary education to the County Councils, authorized them to levy rates for building schools and required them to appoint an Education Committee consisting partly of County Councillors and partly of other 'persons of experience in education and persons acquainted with the needs of the various kinds of schools'.

The chairman of the Cornwall Education Committee for the first twenty years of its existence was R. G. Rows (a farmer and a Methodist local preacher from Helston) and the paid secretary for the first thirty years was F. R. Pascoe, who greatly admired his chairman and worked in close co-operation with him. R. G. Rows, who had already won a reputation as an eloquent speaker in the Liberal cause, was described by Pascoe as the wisest old man he ever knew, 'a real philosopher given to much meditation, whose zeal for education was a consuming fire'. He said that 'his venerable figure, his extraordinary command of language and his deep earnestness often seemed to cow the Council into conviction against its natural inclination'. Pascoe also admired Q greatly. He described him as 'debonair to the eye, always human and witty, with a profound knowledge of what education really is—liable to quote his master, Plato, at every opportunity'. The three men, by their close collaboration, their determination and their optimism, brought about a great change for the better in the Cornish educational system.

At Rows's special request, Q became chairman of the School Management Committee and Pascoe considered that he enjoyed the duties of this office more than any other work he did for the County Council. It involved visits at all times of the year to three hundred or more schools scattered all over Cornwall. Some of them were easily visited, but even these had their problems. Once, for instance (to quote the secretary): 'We crossed from Q's jetty to Polruan in a tempestuous sea to quell a mutiny which had broken out in the boys' school. Q's report—I didn't write a word of it—was a masterpiece, and tranquillity was restored.' Other journeys were to very remote places which, Q said, could be reached only after 'long journeys over many outlandish roads (in days when the motor-car was scarcely known)' and by means of 'every kind of ramshackle hired conveyance'. Yet, in spite of frequent discomforts, he enjoyed these journeys and the long conversations which they entailed with country parsons, school managers and teachers. He never forgot them; and the experience that he gained from them enabled him to plead the cause of elementary education, and to state its difficulties from first-hand knowledge, when delivering lectures to university audiences or when writing for a wide public. In 1920, for instance, in the preface to his *Art of Reading*, he said:

The real battle for English lies in our Elementary Schools, and in the training of our Elementary Teachers....My thoughts have too often strayed from my audience in a University theatre away to remote rural class-rooms where the hungry sheep look up and are not fed; to piteous groups of urchins standing at attention and chanting *The Wreck of the Hesperus* in unison;

and in 1929, in the third volume of his *Studies in Literature*, after pleading for at least an hour's silent reading a day in elementary schools, he said:

Be it remembered, these children have no room, no opportunity, no light as a rule, no table-space, for 'evening preparation', 'home lessons'. Their father returns tired from his day's work and with pardonable gruffness orders them to 'Get out and play'. There is often but one lamp, kept on the move from kitchen to scullery and back; there is no library. I am speaking generally of course, but you know this to be true of hundreds of thousands of children.

Until the Balfour Act of 1902 public bodies had no power to make provision for secondary education and Cornwall was more badly provided with secondary schools than most counties. The Act made it possible for the County Education Committee to remedy this defect and Rows, Q and Pascoe were determined to remedy it as soon as possible. Their object was to build a secondary school within reasonable distance of every house in Cornwall, in spite of its being predominantly a rural county. They had great obstacles to encounter—prejudice, suspicion, sectarian strife, apathy and (particularly at first) direct opposition from many rate-payers and even from County Councillors. They carried on undaunted until they had built a fine chain of secondary schools throughout the county and Rows was able to say with triumph: 'Well, there the schools are: they can't go back to the quarries again.' In later years Q had the great satisfaction of seeing numbers of children go from Cornish elementary schools to the secondary schools and on to the universities, one of them (A. L. Rowse) becoming a Fellow of All Souls.

While Q was carrying out his manifold civic duties he was also working hard in the political sphere to secure the return of South-East Cornwall to the Liberal fold, which it had abandoned in 1895. His wishes were fulfilled at the general election held in January 1906, when the Liberal party won a sweeping victory throughout the country and South-East Cornwall shared in it by returning the Hon. T. C. R. Agar-Robartes to Parliament. Barrie had wanted Q to stand as a candidate in that election but Q had no wish at all for a Parliamentary career. The next general election came in January 1910 and in the campaign which preceded it Q 'caught Radical politics badly', as one newspaper expressed it. 'Q is frightfully busy over the election', Kenneth Grahame wrote to a friend, 'propagating his pernicious doctrines throughout the west country.' The Liberal majority throughout the kingdom was greatly reduced, but South-East Cornwall again returned a Liberal member, C. A. Grenfell. It is no doubt this election that is described in such interesting detail in Q's essay, 'The Election Count', which he included in his *News from the Duchy* in 1913.

Q's combined literary, educational and political services had by this time reached such dimensions that Mr Asquith, who had become Prime Minister in 1908, decided to recognize them by getting him created a knight bachelor. His name accordingly appeared in King George V's first Birthday Honours list, published in June 1910, and on 7 July he was knighted by the King at St James's Palace. It was a popular knighthood and he had to spend a long time afterwards answering letters of congratulation; or, as he put it, 'attempting to wipe up the precious balms with which friends nearly broke my head'. On the day when he returned from London the band of the Fowey Territorials, in whose formation a year or two previously he had played a leading part, welcomed him home by assembling outside The Haven in the evening and playing 'A Fine Old English Gentleman' and other popular melodies. In the autumn the Liberals of Fowey and Lanteglos held a meeting to congratulate him on his title and to make a presentation to him and Lady Quiller-Couch. Political feeling had run high at Fowey as elsewhere in the country for some years; and Q, in returning thanks for the presentation, commented on the 'very queer fate' that had dragged him into politics when his one ambition was to be a man of letters. It had not always been fun to be a Liberal at Fowey, he said; he had been abused and slandered for his politics, but he had exercised courage and self-restraint and feeling was much better now.

In December of the same year there was another general election. The Liberal party went back to Westminster with almost exactly the same majority as in the previous January, but South-East Cornwall this time rejected the Liberal candidate, Isaac Foot, and returned Sir Reginald Pole-Carew, a Conservative. Before the election, Q, on behalf of the Liberal Association for the constituency, had sent a telegram to a distinguished Radical, Leif Jones, asking him to be their candidate; but Leif Jones, having already made promises to stand for another constituency, had to decline. When the election was over he wrote to Q as follows:

Your telegram, suggesting that I should come and fight Bodmin, tempted me very much: for it would have been glorious to have had an election with you as Chairman of the Liberal Association; but I was negotiating about another seat when your telegram arrived, and so the opportunity passed. As it turns out, I could not have won the seat for you. I know Foot: and as he was an excellent local candidate and yet did not win, an outsider like myself could not hope to have done so. I suspect you are the man who can bring the constituency back to the fold. Why don't you come in? and yet I don't know that you should: anybody will make a respectable Liberal member of Parliament, while nobody else can write the books with which you enrich and delight us.

One can scarcely help thinking that Q did not receive Leif Jones's refusal with entirely unmixed feelings. On the one hand, they had been contemporaries at Trinity College, Oxford, and belonged to the same wing of the Liberal party. On the other hand, Leif Jones was a Nonconformist and a teetotaller and Q disliked Nonconformity and detested teetotalism. It is true that, being a Liberal, he belonged to a party of which Nonconformity, the close ally of teetotalism, was the backbone. His life-long fidelity to Liberalism is, indeed, one of many examples of his sacrificing his personal preferences to his deep-seated convictions. Leif Jones, however, was no ordinary teetotaller: he was a militant, who stumped the country preaching teetotalism; and, to crown it all, he was President of the United Kingdom Alliance for the Total Suppression of the Liquor Traffic. The humour of the situation must have appealed to Q, who was never slow to laugh at himself.

The election of December 1910 was the last in which Q took an active part, but he continued to take an interest in politics to the end of his life. In 1912, although he was at the time President of the Liberal Association for his constituency, his humanitarianism prompted him to oppose the Liberal Government openly on its Mental Deficiency Bill. This Bill, which was sponsored by the Home Secretary, Reginald McKenna, proposed that not merely the insane but also the feeble-minded could, if proved incapable of managing their own affairs, be permanently detained in official establishments under government control. It was supported by the Association for the Permanent Care of the Feeble-minded, of which the Bishop of Exeter was a prominent member. The Bill had already passed its second reading when Q published in Hilaire Belloc's weekly, *The Eye-Witness*, three 'Open Letters to the Right Reverend Archibald Robertson, D.D., Lord Bishop of Exeter', in which he used to great effect the correct form of address to a bishop. 'My Lord,' he reminded the Bishop in his first letter, 'you were Dean of our old College at Oxford—the first don from whom, as a raw freshman, I took kindly advice.' In his second letter he said:

My Lord, I have been a writer now these twenty-five years and I cannot remember to have written in that time sentences so vile as those which I am now copying from an Act of Parliament proposed by a Liberal Government—a Government into the cause of which some of us, through three campaigns, flung such energies as men give for the sake of high hopes. Let the hopes be: but our trust, at least, was that liberty to a Liberal Government was as chastity to a woman. Of each it is true that, once broken, it descends by easier and yet easier lapses to the standard of a strumpet, or of Mr McKenna;

and in his third letter:

My Lord,...Your predecessor in the cathedral throne of Exeter provoked a smile when he went down and confirmed a number of inmates of the Starcross Asylum. The smile widened when, being a very simple sincere man, he explained (I forget the exact words) that in his experience persons of weak intellect were peculiarly amenable to the Christian Faith. The laugh was cheap and came easy. Yet I rather choose to remember with how sweet a charity for centuries the poor folk of Europe have suffered and fed their half-wits, naming them 'God's fools'. Ponder that name, my lord.

The Bill was withdrawn before the third reading. When it was re-introduced in the following year it was in a different form.

Q was still President of the South-East Cornwall Liberal Association when, in October 1912, he was interviewed by the newly founded *Daily Citizen*—the first official daily organ of the Labour Party. He welcomed the new periodical. 'I do want', he said, 'to see a paper that will give honest, liberal opinions without the taint of capital upon it—a paper that will give the opinions of a liberal mind on public affairs. I don't care whether it is a Labour paper or one of any other political colour. I sympathize with Labour, and am with them all the time.' In the same interview he stated his intention of withdrawing from public life. 'I have had twelve years of public life', he said, 'and am getting to the age, I think, when a man should retire on the philosophic life. I want to get out of the hurly-burly and look at it from a distance, so that I may have leisure to write down some conclusions I have come to which can be expressed more freely by a retired man, because in the first place he will not be suspected of having any particular axe to grind and secondly he can talk without compromising his own political friends.'

A few weeks after this interview it became clear that Q would have to live at least half the year away from Cornwall in future. This strengthened his determination to retire from public life, at least to the extent that he resigned the presidency of the Liberal Association. If by 'public life' he had meant anything more than politics it is clear that he had changed his mind, either voluntarily or under pressure, for he retained his other offices. Despite the sentiments which he had expressed in the *Daily Citizen*, he declared that he remained 'a better Liberal than ever'. Although in later years he sometimes voted for the Labour Party if there was no Liberal candidate, he never left the Liberal Party. His loyalty was such that the more deeply the Liberal ship sank, the less inclined he became to leave it.

Kenneth Grahame, who did not share Q's political views, revisited Fowey in 1911, accompanied by his wife and youthful son, Alastair, who was nicknamed 'Mouse'. Q naturally took them, as he took most of his guests, to visit the small piece of land that he had acquired in 1904 on the far side of the harbour. He called it jocularly 'The Farm', which became its usual name in the family. It had been the garden of a disused tavern called 'Priam's Cellars', the ruins of which still stand just above the landing place. Q derived great pleasure from 'The Farm' and until he died he rowed over the harbour to it almost daily when he was at home.

Grahame had accepted the dedication of *The Mayor of Troy* in 1906 with the remark: 'I feel now really officially connected with the place, through its Mayor, and some day I shall put in for an almshouse, if you have any.' When he revisited Fowey in May 1911 he wrote to Austin Purves—a Philadelphia business man who had first been attracted to Fowey by Q's writings and became a frequent visitor—that on the whole the place had not changed much. It was true, he said, that the china clay was now loaded on to the ships by electricity, day and night, and that new houses had been built; but the old town and the harbour front were the same as ever. He continued:

Also the same Q, looking not a day older and even more beautifully dressed than formerly. Mouse was particularly struck with Q's clothes. I think he then realized, for the first time, that Man, when he chooses to give his mind to it, is incomparably the finer animal of the two and does the greater justice to his clothes.... The farm—'Priam's Cellars'—flourishes exceedingly. One sunny day we all went over there with a large luncheon basket and lunched in the open... in a riot of daffodils and primroses, with three big foreign ships—Danes and Norwegians—moored right below us.

A few weeks after the Grahames' visit to Fowey Q was busy helping with the local celebration of the coronation of King George V, which took place on 22 June. It was carried out on much the same lines as in 1902. The local newspaper, in its report of the morning service at the parish church, tells us that 'the sacred old edifice was filled to overflowing', that two military bands accompanied the singing and that 'the choir rendered Sir Arthur Quiller-Couch's hymn, *Of old our city hath renown*'. Immediately after the service Lady Quiller-Couch and Mrs Purcell, the wife of the Vicar of Fowey, each planted a red chestnut-tree just outside the church door; and (to quote the local paper again) 'a *feu de joie* was then fired, and considering the men had very little chance of practising it they did it with really decent precision'. In the evening, while coloured lights twinkled on every house-front, on the arches that here and there spanned the narrow main street, and on the shipping in the harbour, 'a ball was held in the Armoury, the lead being taken by Sir Arthur and Lady Quiller-Couch, and the majority of the dancers being in fancy costumes of brilliant colours'. Earlier in the evening Q had contributed to the day's programme an item that had been lacking from the celebrations of 1902. Historical pageants had come into fashion since then and Q had sketched one for the ancient city of Merchester in his *Brother Copas*. The coronation of George V gave him the opportunity of writing a real one for Fowey. He called it *This Royal Throne of Kings*, modestly describing it, not as a pageant, but as a children's masque. It provided, said the local paper, 'a truly royal entertainment, the like of which was not beaten this side of Bristol'.

Some of the stage properties required in the masque were designed by Bevil Quiller-Couch, who was an undergraduate at Oxford by this time. He entered Trinity College in January 1910 and was in residence until the summer of 1913. Though not his father's equal in intellectual ability, he possessed his personal charm and keen sense of humour and excelled him as an athlete. Q was very pleased when Bevil and a son of his old friend Gilbert Coleridge rowed in a Trinity boat together and were coached by Gilbert Coleridge. Bevil went on to stroke two University Trial Eights and won the University Pairs two years running. He had inherited his father's love for boats of every kind and in 1911 spent a good deal of his summer vacation yachting, sometimes with undergraduate friends, sometimes with the commodore of the Fowey Yacht Club, Edward Atkinson. In September, when he and Atkinson were sailing a twelve-foot boat off the coast near Fowey, the vessel foundered in a heavy sea. Bevil managed to swim ashore to a small cove, supporting Atkinson, who was unconscious. He climbed the rocks with a great effort to summon help, but before the rescue party could arrive Atkinson had been washed out to sea, from which his dead body was recovered when the weather had calmed again. Q had been very fond of Atkinson, to whom he had dedicated *Lady Good-for-Nothing* a year before. He succeeded him as commodore of the Fowey Yacht Club and held the office till he died.

Q naturally visited Oxford more frequently while his son was in residence than he had done ever since 1887 and his visits brought him back prominently into the notice of his old friends and contemporaries, among whom were R. W. Raper, Bursar of Trinity, and T. H. Warren, President of Magdalen. The Professorship of Poetry, which was filled by election every five years, was due to fall vacant early in 1911. It was a spare-time post, capable of being held by a non-resident; and on 24 December 1910, Raper wrote to Q as follows:

> Would you be willing to be nominated, if I can arrange it, for the Professorship of Poetry which is vacant some time soon? Pay small, duties light (lecture twice a term at most, I think), honour great. It may involve a contest, say with Beeching or someone else. There is a move to get Bradley to stand again but many would rather try someone else.
>
> I believe the usual way is for twelve representative people to join together and nominate. Warren as an old Cliftonian should help.

According to Q, Warren said definitely that he would support him if he were a candidate. He therefore agreed to stand; but when he arrived at Oxford to inquire into the formalities of the election Warren told him he had decided to be a candidate himself. Q thereupon retired from the contest and at the election in February 1911 Warren secured a majority of votes over H. C. Beeching. He and Q met again next year—whether either of them felt any embarrassment we do not know—when they, together with Henry Newbolt, received honorary degrees from the University of Bristol on the same day.

Meanwhile, in the very month in which Warren became Professor of Poetry at Oxford, Cambridge received its first Professor of English Literature. In November 1910 Sir Harold Harmsworth (afterwards Lord Rothermere), the newspaper magnate, had offered £20,000 to the University for the foundation of a new professorship. The conditions attached to the offer were that the professorship should be named in memory of King Edward VII, that each Professor should be nominated by the Crown and that 'it should be the duty of the Professor to deliver courses on English Literature from the age of Chaucer onwards, and otherwise to promote, so far as may be in his power, the study in the University of the subject of English Literature'. A further stipulation was that 'the Professor shall treat this subject on literary and critical rather than on philological and linguistic lines'. The offer was accepted by the University, but there was some opposition. When details of tenure were being discussed later in the Senate Dr J. M. E. M'Taggart (Q's contemporary at Clifton) said that 'it seemed to him that a Professorship of such a subject, and to be filled up in such a manner, would not only be useless but positively harmful to the University'. The comments of another member of the Senate, Dr J. Mayo, were summarized in the *Cambridge University Reporter* as follows:

What was the natural conclusion to be drawn from the position with regard to this Professorship? Why, that the University must be so ignorant of the value of English Literature that it required a bequest of £20,000 to deliver them from their state of ignorance. The imputation of ignorance of English Literature was certainly cast upon them by an offer of that kind. For his part, he felt that the offer was dictated by the most generous and praiseworthy spirit, but a totally ignorant one. What he was afraid of was that this Professorship...would be simply a Professorship of English Literature dating from the beginning of the latter half of the nineteenth century, and the effect of that would be that it would be a Professorship of English fiction, and that of a light and comic character. For that reason, he thought that the Professorship was a Professorship unworthy of the University.

The Senate nevertheless approved of the proposed conditions of tenure and on 20 February 1911 the Vice-Chancellor gave notice that Arthur Woolgar Verrall, a classical scholar and a Fellow of Trinity College, had been appointed the first holder of the chair. He was admitted to office three days later and delivered his inaugural lecture on 10 May. Already an invalid who had to be wheeled into the lecture room in a chair, he died on 18 June 1912, after only sixteen months in office.

The vacancy had not been filled when a new academical year began in the autumn and accordingly *The Cambridge Review* of 17 October said:

Perhaps the Prime Minister will not resent the reminder that we are still without a King Edward VII Professor of English Literature and the suggestion that the King, in whose gift the Professorship is, may be waiting for his advice. We know that there are other matters to occupy Mr Asquith's attention, and the University has indeed managed to make shift for some centuries without a Professor of English Literature. Still, this is the era of the *Daily Mail* and a Professor is sorely needed. Rumour says that a Cabinet Minister may be appointed to the post and leaves us wondering which of two it will be. *Obiter Dicta* might perhaps fall in best with the founder's idea of avoiding pedantry, while another Minister has qualified by a severer study of Wordsworth, sandwiched in between biographies of English statesmen of the eighteenth and nineteenth centuries. How happy could we be with either if Mr Asquith would only decide!

If the Prime Minister took this hint and offered the chair to either Augustine Birrell or Lord Morley he must have received a refusal, for on 31 October the Vice-Chancellor informed the University that Sir Arthur Quiller-Couch had been appointed King Edward VII Professor of English Literature.

Some years later, when Q was making an after-lunch speech at Cambridge, he said: 'I speak, gentlemen, as a Professor of English Literature—what is more, as a King Edward VII Professor of English Literature. Tax not *that* royal saint with vain expense.'

CHAPTER VI

FIRST YEARS AT CAMBRIDGE (1912-14)

THE Prime Minister's offer of the King Edward VII Professorship had startled Q. If he had ever before heard of the existence of the chair he had forgotten it, he said; and the death of Verrall had been to him, as to others, 'of concern mainly as the untimely loss to his country of a brilliant classical scholar'.

Other people were equally startled and one can understand their feelings. After all, Q had produced no substantial work of English literary criticism, and his classical scholarship—one could not help comparing him with Verrall—was represented only by an Introduction to the *Pervigilium Veneris* in 1911 and a Swinburnesque translation of it published only two months before his appointment to Cambridge. He was known to an increasing number as a discriminating anthologist but to most people only as a writer of fiction, so that Dr Mayo and his friends must have felt entitled to say, 'We told you so.' Some of the extreme Conservatives, for their part, regarded his appointment as purely political.

There were nevertheless others, even in academic circles, who approved of it. *The Cambridge Review*, for instance, considered it 'the most popular which could possibly have been made'. A. C. Benson, though he did not yet know Q well, was quick to realize that he possessed many of the qualities that would be of particular value to the as yet unborn school of English literature in the University, and his letter of welcome to Q ran:

Dear Sir Arthur,

I have read with great interest to-night of your appointment here as our new Professor of English Literature, and write to congratulate you most heartily. It is a really great opportunity. There are many men here interested in literature, but there is no centralization. What we want is a man who will really found and organize a *school*. Everything is ready for this, and what is needed is a strong personality, to do for us just what Raleigh has done at Oxford; and this I hope and believe you will do.... You will be much welcomed here, and I think you will find all the materials ready to your hand. It is not only stimulating teaching that is wanted, it is a social centre for individual energies. I am sure you will be a real force here, and I shall confidently look forward to seeing a school of literature take shape in your hands.

Another prominent member of the University to express approval of the appointment was Henry Jackson, the Professor of Greek, who wrote to Q: 'I have to confess that I had not thought of you for the post. I suppose that I was blind, not being able to imagine you away from Fowey. But this makes me applaud all the more the happy thought, whose soever it may have been.... I was able to tell Runciman last night of the universal popularity of the appointment.'

Q valued such letters as these greatly because, being by nature a shy man and not having lectured for a quarter of a century—and then only to a small college audience—he contemplated his new work with some anxiety. He wrote to Henry Jackson:

I am in a hideous funk over it all; and the hopeless sense of ignorance and incompetence will only never be believed because (I hope) it will never be seen.
But it's this way: I do want to make a brave effort....
I want to be useful and make a job of it—if that's at all inside my range—and not to waste time in preparing show lectures the hollowness of which you would all precious soon detect.
I take it that what you want—after I have sat down and learnt a bit—is someone to go to work quietly and sweat at a School of English Literature. If that be so, I shall want all your advice....
My notion is—all this has happened so suddenly—to come up some time in November and take counsel with those best able to give it: to look about for a temporary home; and to lay plans to get the work started on right lines with the Lent Term. Flourishes like the Inaugural etc. must take care of themselves.

His appointment to a Professorship carried with it membership of the University but not of any of its component colleges. There was, however, a likelihood that one or more of them would invite him to join them; and, if not, he could himself make advances. If accepted for membership he could then, being a Master of Arts of Oxford, be admitted to the same degree at Cambridge 'by incorporation'. With this in mind, his old political associate, Leonard Courtney—Lord Courtney of Penwith since 1906—wrote to him on 4 November, putting the case for various colleges, including the one of which he himself had been a member. He said:

I must send you a word to express my great pleasure in thinking you are coming over to help younger generations at Cambridge. I hail the migration as a very happy one.

I suppose bye and bye you will be 'incorporated', and as in private duty bound I desire your consideration of the ancient foundation of St John's, the nursing home of Herrick, Mat Prior and William Wordsworth, if not of Ben Jonson, beside a galaxy of stars of the second magnitude from Robert Greene down to Domett and poor Thomas Ashe. You may perhaps be seduced by the splendours of Trinity with Dryden, Byron and Tennyson, though if not drawn to St John's I should myself have a kindly thought of Pembroke with Spenser and Gray, though some would doubtless declare that Milton is an irresistible magnet to Christ's. To go back to St John's, let me remind you how you would specially find yourself at home in the college of Henry Martin, Colenso and John Couch Adams.*

Lord Courtney had overlooked Jesus College, which had produced Cranmer, Laurence Sterne and Coleridge; but Q had already received from that college an offer, not of mere incorporation, but of a Fellowship—the professorial Fellowship vacated by Dr W. R. Inge when he left Cambridge for London in the previous year to become Dean of St Paul's. This offer was conveyed in the first official letter that the new Master of the College, Arthur Gray, had written since his election to office a few days before. Q accepted it and was formally elected a Fellow of Jesus College on 7 November. On the 9th, when he was at Cambridge, he was admitted to his Fellowship and also to his Professorship. During this visit he stayed in the rooms that had been allotted to him

* Three Cornishmen.

for his permanent use in the second court at Jesus College and he found them depressing. This was chiefly because the windows (being on the ground floor and opening on to the Close) were fitted with iron bars. This made him feel like a prisoner: at Fowey, for twenty years past, he had looked through unbarred windows on to the open sea.

One of the Fellows of the College who had been unable to be present at the ceremony of Q's admission was Mr (afterwards Sir) Sydney Cockerell, who had corresponded with him at intervals for a number of years. Q wrote to him from Fowey on 24 November:

It is a long time that I have owed you a letter: but first of all I promised myself the pleasure of meeting and thanking you at Jesus College. They were all amazingly kind to me—and I cannot tell you how proud I am to belong to that Society—but I looked round in search of you, et quum interrogatum est 'Ubi est ille S. C. Cockerell?' statim responsum est ab omnibus—as on a previous occasion reported by De Quincey—'Non est inventus.'

Well, there will be time! My wife and I propose to come up to Cambridge early next month, house-hunting: and I am already deep in a correspondence with people about lectures, etc. next term. Meanwhile it will be of interest to you to know that the *Oxford Book of Victorian Verse* is billed to be published next week, and I have vainly tried to express my gratitude to you in the preface. I want—after the manner of grateful persons—to use your kindness still further, by asking your advice on one or two points 'connected with' the Chair.

I am in a dreadful funk, of course, but marching forward (like the British infantry in the Peninsula) with my eyes shut.

When *The Oxford Book of Victorian Verse* appeared shortly afterwards it bore the dedication: 'To my future friends and pupils at Cambridge, this propitiatory wreath.' Q stated in the preface that he had followed his old rule of choosing what seemed to him the best, and for that reason alone. 'The reader', he said, 'will allow me to pursue my old rule to the end; and when he re-greets in this volume many a poem that adorned the former one he will understand that by excluding these I should have condemned myself to anthologizing the second-rate and clearing the ground for an *Oxford Book of the Worst Poetry*—which, by the way, might be a not unentertaining work.'

The Cambridge Review liked this preface and suggested that if his lectures were up to the same level, or to the level of his novels, Cambridge had 'a series of treats in store'.

In January 1913 Q went officially into residence at Cambridge. Lady Quiller-Couch and he had already decided that they could not bear to leave Fowey permanently and make their home at Cambridge all the year round. They hoped to find a small house in which they could live at Cambridge during term, returning to Fowey for the vacations. Meanwhile, they lived in rooms in Thompson's Lane.

On 17 January he received the honorary degree of Master of Arts in the Senate House. The Public Orator, Sir John Sandys, who presented him, neatly summed up his career in his Latin speech, which ended with a reflection on the appropriateness of Q's becoming a Fellow of Laurence Sterne's old college:

Professoris nostri primi in locum Regis nomine missus nobis est Arthurus alter, Regis Arthuri prope regionem fabulosam natus, vir in Athenis illis Oxoniensibus et litterarum humaniorum et fluminis Isis amore olim insignis, qui Collegii sui inter praeceptores paulisper numeratus, primum viam Londiniensem vocantem audivit, deinde ad solum natale reversus, portus olim celeberrimi in litore et vitae suae tabernaculum et scriptorum suorum complurium argumentum invenit. Ibi Troiae novae Homerus novus constitutus, pedestri in sermone quot opera de personis fictis conscripsit!...Iuvat denique ad artis criticae experimenta illa priora reverti, in quibus ea quae de poetis Cantabrigiensibus, ipse poeta Oxoniensis, lepide conscripsit, ne Cantabrigiensibus quidem displicere possunt. Opere in eodem contra censores quosdam nimium severos fortiter defendit operum duorum immortalium scriptorem amabilem Laurentium Sterne. Laetamur alumni tanti a Collegio eximio Professorem nostrum novum, Professoris nomine, socium esse electum.

On 29 January he delivered his inaugural lecture in the newly built lecture theatre at the Arts School. Scorning to appear in the heterogeneous clothing normally worn for lecturing at Cambridge, he had put on correct morning dress, as he did for all subsequent lectures to the end of his life. The lecture theatre was packed with an uncounted but overflowing audience—'that curious audience, almost as interesting as Q himself', as one who was present afterwards called it. It included old and young; male and female; dons from the Vice-Chancellor downwards, under-graduates and visitors; and it overflowed from the closely packed benches on to the floor and the window ledges.

He began his inaugural lecture, as he began all his lectures, nervously, but it was as carefully prepared and arranged as the clothes he wore: not a word of it was out of place. He delivered it in the quiet, gentle, dignified voice that he always used, whether in conversation or in lecturing. If Dr Mayo and his friends were present they must have been somewhat embarrassed to find that the lecturer began with a reference, not to Stevenson, Rider Haggard, or Barry Pain, but to Plato. As he went on, he showed how steeped he still was in the Classics, even though he had neither lectured on them for a quarter of a century nor had had time to study them systematically. The lecture overflowed with Q's humanity, his good taste and his humour, and at a stroke made him what he remained to the end—a leading figure in the life of the University.

The lectures that followed at fortnightly intervals showed the same wide knowledge of the Classics as the first and possessed the same classical restraint and common sense. They revealed the same desire to encourage their hearers to link theory with practice, they were enlivened by the same shafts of humour and they continued to attract much larger audiences than any other lectures in Cambridge. The first dozen of them, collected into a volume called *On the Art of Writing*, became as well known as *The Oxford Book of English Verse*. Their thesis, Q said,

amounts to this—Literature is not a mere Science, to be studied; but an Art, to be practised. Great as is our own literature, we must consider it as a legacy to be improved. Any nation that potters with any glory of its past, as a thing dead and done for, is to that extent renegade. If that be granted, not all our pride in a Shakespeare can excuse the relaxation of an effort—however vain and hopeless—to better him, or some part of him. If, with all our native exemplars to give us courage, we persist in striving to write well, we can easily resign to other nations all the secondary fame to be picked up by commentators.

One very remarkable feature of his lectures was that they lost none of their force or charm when put into print. 'It was magical to hear his lectures delivered', says one of his old pupils (Canon Roger Lloyd), 'and this magic had some alchemy distilled into it which carried it unimpaired over the awkward transition from the spoken to the written word. The result was and is that Q's hearers and his readers were at once brought under a kind of compulsion to read for themselves the great works he was describing.'

His invariable practice of addressing his audience as 'Gentlemen', even though it always included women and even though the women were often in a majority, gave rise to the legend that he objected to their presence at his lectures. If it had been so, he could have refused admission to all women other than the members of Girton and Newnham Colleges, but he did nothing of the kind. On the contrary, he admitted everyone who cared to attend, whether they were men or women, and he frequently did this against the wishes of the administrative staff of the University, whose duty it was to see that outsiders did not attend lectures without special permission. He also admitted women as freely as men to his informal evening discussions, from which (as he was not compelled to hold them) he could have excluded even the members of the two women's colleges if he had wished. He addressed his audiences as 'Gentlemen' because he believed in being strictly correct on formal occasions, as he showed by the very dress he wore. In theory, he was lecturing to members of the University only; and, since the women's colleges were not legally included in the University, he maintained that it would be incorrect for him to include them in his form of address. The women who were present understood all this and, far from resenting his manner of beginning his lectures, rather enjoyed it.

'Gentlemen'

Another legend, which grew almost inevitably out of the first, asserted that at one of his lectures there was only one man in the audience and that Q consequently began with 'Sir'; and that on another occasion, when the audience was composed entirely of women, he began with no form of address at all and spoke as if he were meditating aloud. One version of this story, circulated by an American Professor who was at Cambridge for a year, asserted that Q's usual form of address was 'Young Gentlemen' and that when only one man was present in the audience it became 'Young Gentleman'. It is curious that the author of an admirable, and in all other respects accurate, study of English life during the war of 1939–45 should have imagined that such forms of address were possible in England.

In addition to his formal lectures, which were always delivered at noon and generally on Wednesdays, Q held classes once or twice a week. For many years they were held in the room which the University had allotted to him for professorial use in the Divinity School, opposite St John's College, and began at 8.30 in the evening. In later years they were transferred to the Arts School or to Jesus College, but began at the same hour. During the war years from 1939 to his death, when the blackout made evening meetings difficult, he held them at noon on Saturdays, at Jesus College. They were always quite informal. Q, who was an inveterate smoker, himself set the example of smoking at these meetings and provided cigarettes and coffee for his guests. As happened at his lectures, dons attended as well as undergraduates, among them being A. C. Benson (afterwards Master of Magdalene), Edward Bullough (afterwards Professor of Italian) and Eustace Tillyard (afterwards Master of Jesus). Sometimes members of the class would read papers and Q would lead the discussion that followed. A. C. Benson mentions one of these gatherings in his diary on 4 December 1913:

Went to Quiller-Couch's symposium—about forty men, all round the room, smoking and whispering. Two little papers were read, and I liked the calm humorous way in which Quiller-Couch raised points. I shudder to think of doing it, but he did it well.

Generally, however, the gatherings were advertised in the University lecture list as classes on Aristotle's *Poetics* or on 'The Background of the English Moralists: Aristotle's *Ethics*', which were read in translation. Q would read a passage aloud and then discuss and illustrate it at length. There were many digressions; but these, even if they had little to do with Aristotle, had a most stimulating effect on his hearers, being often enriched—to quote his old pupil, H. S. Bennett—'by a series of observations full of mature wisdom and instinct with humanity'.

A digression which was forced on Q on one occasion provided a particularly good example of his skill in enlisting the sympathy of his audience. 'He had been commenting', one of his pupils says, 'on Aristotle's thesis that comedy is an imitation of men worse than the average. His words were interrupted by a sudden noise of undergraduate revelry from the street outside. Another lecturer might have broken off embarrassed, feeling suddenly remote from his hearers, instinctively assuming that these would as it were take sides with the crowd outside and against himself. Not so Q. He broke off his lecture and, joining himself to his audience, remarked: "Gentlemen, let us pause and listen to men worse than ourselves".'

As a Professor, Q was not required to give individual tuition—'supervision', as it is called at Cambridge—to undergraduates, but he sometimes did so. He frequently supervised the work of men doing research for the degree of Doctor of Philosophy when it was instituted after the war of 1914–18, and he occasionally supervised ordinary undergraduates out of pure compassion. His first pupil was an undergraduate of St John's College, W. A. Darlington, afterwards well known as a dramatic critic, who found him a very thorough supervisor. 'He read everything I wrote', he said, 'and mostly made me write it again.'

Q was always ready to help any undergraduate who called on him at his rooms in Jesus College for advice about his work, unless he called without an appointment during the morning or between tea and dinner—those being the times when he did most of his writing. Anyone who paid a casual call during those hours would get no reply to his first two or three knocks. About the fourth knock Q would begin to express his feelings aloud, without fully realizing what he was doing, and at that point the caller would sometimes run away. If he stood his ground he would in due course be invited inside. After the summer of 1914, when Q no longer had his family at Cambridge and lived entirely in college during term, the uninstructed were apt to call on him before he had breakfasted. Anyone who did so was particularly unwelcome. Q would receive him in his dressing-gown and after asking him to take a seat would disappear into his bedroom, from which half-suppressed mutterings would emerge. He would re-appear with a doleful face at frequent intervals to ask questions, wearing one more garment at each re-appearance. Finally, he would make an appointment for a future meeting, upon which the caller would withdraw.

His celebrated Interlude on Jargon, which immediately became a classic, was delivered on 1 May 1913. He used its theme again a few weeks later in a sketch called 'Voices from the Bank' that he contributed to the May-Week number of *The Cambridge Review*. The 'voices' include those of Venator and Piscator, Gorgo and Praxinoë, Dr Johnson and Boswell, Socrates and Adeimantus, Aunts and Cousins, and a Professor of Jargon, who is heard saying:

The races at Oxford and at Cambridge, while partaking in general of a similar character, are rowed under somewhat diverse conditions respectively. In the case of the former University the boats in all cases are of a uniform nature: in that of the latter a distinction is observed, those of the first division being rowed in boats of carvel construction, while the second is identified rather with the clinker build, in which the strakes have an overlapping tendency. Cases have occurred in which a so-called sandwich boat, having won its way to superior rank, finds itself matched against boats appertaining to that rank which owing to their construction are *ipso facto* of a speedier character. In that case the C.U.B.C.—

At this point a band breaks in with

The flowers that bloom in the spring, tra, la,
Have nothing to do with the case;

and soon afterwards the voice of an easily recognizable Cambridge poet of the time is heard reciting:

> The sort of grass they grow at Grassy
> Is esculent but hardly classy;

> The sort of grass they grow at Ditton
> Is classier, but vile to sit on.

> Th' inhabitants of local inns
> Commit unmentionable sins.

> The ordinances of Long Reach
> Are mostly honoured in the breach.

After May Week that summer the family went home to Fowey for the Long Vacation. They paid a visit to Henley Regatta in July to cheer Jesus College for the Grand Challenge Cup, Trinity College, Oxford, for the Ladies' Plate, and Bevil (who had just finished his career at Oxford) for the Silver Goblets. In the autumn they took part in the festivities that were held when Fowey became a borough for the second time in its history. The town had kept its ancient charter of incorporation until the nineteenth century but had ceased to exercise its privileges after the Reform Act of 1832 and had been formally deprived of them in 1883. The revival of the charter was mainly due to the efforts of Q and Charles Treffry. Q, as President of the Fowey Mercantile Association, drafted a petition asking the Crown to make Fowey a borough again. A Local Government Board inquiry was held early in 1912 and the petition was granted in the autumn of that year. Q afterwards said that 'wise audacity' helped Fowey to get what it wanted at a time when very much larger towns were petitioning in vain to be made boroughs. There can be little or no doubt, however, that the fame which Q had brought to Fowey by his writings, coupled with the benevolent attitude of the President of the Local Government Board, John Burns, contributed even more than audacity to the success of the petition. In October 1913 the Member of Parliament for South-East Cornwall, Sir Reginald

Pole-Carew, formally handed over a new charter to Charles
Treffry, the first mayor of the revived borough. The ceremony
took place under a chestnut tree at Place; and Q made a speech in
which he said: 'Although our streets are narrow, our minds may
be broad enough to keep our sense of proportion, and to remember
that our borough is too small to allow of quarrellings, whether
religious or political, or to admit any other rivalry save in the
service of Fowey.'

A few days later the family went up to Cambridge for the
Michaelmas term—not to the lodgings that they had rented in
Thompson's Lane since January but to a house in Chesterton Lane
which Q had taken on a yearly tenancy and to which they brought
their servants from Fowey. It lay under the shadow of the Castle
Mound and was called 'St Andrew's'. Their neighbours were
Professor and Mrs W. R. Sorley on one side and a small com-
munity of Anglican nuns on the other.

It was with great pleasure that, at the beginning of the same
term, Q moved his college furniture from the second court of
Jesus College to 'C' staircase in the first court. This staircase forms
part of a seventeenth-century range, the rest of the buildings in the
court (which has one side open to the Close) being medieval.
There were two sets of rooms on each of the three floors. On the
ground floor there were the undergraduates' Common Room and
a set of rooms for one undergraduate. On the middle floor Q
occupied the set of rooms at the end of the range and had a lecture
room facing him. Both sets of rooms on the top floor were
occupied by F. J. Foakes-Jackson, one of the outstanding figures in
the life of the University, who had been Dean of the college since
1895.

Q liked his new rooms so much that he kept them until he died
just over thirty years later. His accommodation could not, however, be called luxurious. He had only one good room—his
'keeping-room'—which ran the whole width of the building and
had a door at each of its four corners. One door opened straight
on to the staircase without any kind of lobby, and the others
opened into three small rooms. The first of these was his bedroom,

71

which was only just wide enough to provide space for his bedstead with a chair beside it but looked on to the Close, with its chestnuts and cherry trees. The second was a gyp-room—little more than a big cupboard—in which he kept his cutlery, china and wine. The third was a bathroom, with a deep square bath which had only cold water laid on: hot water had to be brought in cans from the keeping-room fire or carried across the court from the kitchen.

The keeping-room, which became well known to many hundreds of visitors, had three windows. Two of these gave a pleasant view of First Court and a glimpse into the Fellows' Garden on its far side. The third window, at the other end of the room, was next to the fire-place, in which a fire burned all day, even in summer. Over the fire-place hung a low, wide looking-glass, round the frame of which numerous cards were always stuck—notices of meetings of University committees, the Cornwall Education Committee, the Tywardreath Petty Sessions, the Royal Fowey Yacht Club, the County Council, the Imperial Society of Knights Bachelor, the Cambridge University Cruising Club, invitations to college feasts, terminal programmes of graduate or undergraduate societies. Along one side of the room ran a long bookcase, about shoulder high, with a model of the bust of Hermes by Praxiteles standing on it. Against the opposite wall stood a sideboard and a small table. Some of the chairs had arms but there was never an upholstered easy chair or a settee in his rooms at any time. The floor was covered with a brightly coloured Turkey carpet that outlasted his tenancy of the rooms. On it stood the big table at which he worked with his back to the fire. On the table, always exactly in their proper places, lay a collection of small articles, such as an ivory paper-knife marked with a 'Q', a seal at the end of a gold chain, a big fat stick of sealing-wax, a silver cigarette-box, a pile of note-paper, and the pen with which he had failed to get a first class at Oxford and with which (being determined to make good with it) he wrote all his numerous books from *Dead Man's Rock* to *Memories and Opinions*. Two tall vases of flowers always stood close to him on the table, the other end of

Q's Keeping-room at Jesus College, Cambridge

which was occupied by a big bowl of flowers. Another bowlful stood on the sideboard and vases of flowers were dotted all along the top of the bookcase. His return to Cambridge each term was heralded by the arrival of masses of flowers ordered by telegram from a florist in the town. In the May term, when his favourite flower, the peony, was in bloom, there were peonies in all the bowls and vases and also in jugs standing here and there on the floor. Everything in the room reflected the perfect tidiness of its tenant; and the more observant of his visitors noticed the expression of mingled pain, astonishment and pity that came over his face if anyone flicked ash on to his spotless hearth instead of putting it carefully over the top of the fire-guard into the flames.

During the autumn term of 1913 Q continued, as *The Cambridge Review* put it, 'to delight and instruct large audiences by his fortnightly lectures'. These included two lectures 'On the Lineage of English Literature', in which he emphasized the Romance element in English literature and minimized the Germanic. In this term he celebrated his fiftieth birthday. His taste in dress had changed but little since his undergraduate days—it never changed much at any time—and the Jesus College magazine, *Chanticlere*, was able to jest about it in 'A College Alphabet', in which he appeared with such other members of the College as Foakes-Jackson, Gwillym Lloyd George (a freshman that term) and the Chaplain, Edward Wynn (afterwards Bishop of Ely):

F. stands for Foakey, the galloping Dean;
If you go to his chapels you'll know what I mean.

G. is for Gwillym, who pays for his brekker
With funds that accrue from the country's exchequer.

Q. is 'Q' (in the late Verrall's boots):
His bedder plays draughts on his cast-away suits.

W.'s Wynn, who smiles—so angelic!
His intoning in chapel is not strictly melic.

73

First years at Cambridge (1912–14)

Q found time to write now and then for *Chanticlere* himself and in the spring of 1914 there appeared in it some light verse in which he offered jocular advice to an imaginary undergraduate:

AVUNCULAR

Frederic, since your parents twain
At considerable strain
Have packed you hither, here to spend
Three expensive years on end
(Myself contributing a share),
That thereafter you may wear,
As learning fosters Natural Parts,
A Baccalaureate of Arts—
Accept some Rules whereby to steer
An Undergraduate career.

Benefactors who designed
Colleges to bless their kind,
Building chapels, planting trees,
Lavishing amenities,
Plann'd not, in these fair resorts,
Stadia for athletic sports.
Had they done so, it is odds
Cambridge courts and Oxford quads
Had been fashioned not so small;
Nay ('tis likely) not at all.

Within our studious cloisters' pale
(So different from Sunningdale),
Abstain from golfing, or to toss
The caber (Scottish), or Lacrosse
(Indo-Canadian), or to play
At base-ball pitching (U.S.A.)—
Nay, tho' the Fox- or Steeple-chase
Better demean our Island race,
Spare from the tutelary Pump
To irrigate a water-jump:

First years at Cambridge (1912–14)

And—O, my Frederic!—in the Chimney*
Do not at risk of life or limb ne-
gotiate its double wall
In practice for the National;
Nor to our inmost Academe
Import a rival Rugger team;
Nor beagle, nor on Polo ponies
Trespass in pursuit of conies.

While in Hall the Grace is said
Do not use your daily bread
For missiles, nor, to gain your seat,
Tread the napery with your feet.
Solecisms such as these
May in neighb'ring colleges
Find a plea in use and wont,
But at Jesus Coll. they don't (?).

Prowess of aquatic crews
Licensed revel may excuse:
But don't reward the Tutor's boon
With nihilism by maroon:
Nor deem the purpose of a bon-
fire's to put the Dean upon.
You may cook him to a turn
For heresy, and after learn
You've artistically browned
One of orthodoxy sound.
(An error by historians blamed
On Bishop Bonner—aptly named.)

When to Learning's sacred Porch
On a motor-bike you scorch,
Avoid the ambients to trace
Of Portugal's seductive Place,
And of one funeral make a brace

* The name given to the walled path that connects the inner and outer
gates of Jesus College.

By cutting through it at the corner
And boosting some belated mourner
(A trick by Naval Experts much
Applauded as 'the Nelson touch'),
Merely to prove that your machine's
Interior is full of beans:
Nor glut its homicidal fury
With holocausts in Petty Cury.
(Petty Cury's denizen
Has his rights, like other men;
Though he be obscene to view,
Heav'n made *him* as well as *you*).
Forty miles an hour or so
Is as fast as you should go.
Loftier locomotive feats
Reserve for less congested streets.

Should th' allurements of the Stage
Your eupeptic hours engage,
And Shaw's or Gilbert's sock be on,
Don't exhort the histrion:
Nor to the *coryphée* discover
In public that She Made You Love Her,
Nor with endearing terms applaud her.
With like restraint, should Harry Lauder
Impersonate the Royal Dane,
Or Romeo, or Scotia's thane,
Forbear to intimate that you
Could do what he essays to do.
Demonstrable though it be,
Keep it for the A.D.C.

Frederic, these Rules forgive
For being mostly negative!
'Tis by self-effacing ways
Studious boys deserve the bays
And at length become B.A.'s.

At the end of the summer term that year the family went back
to Fowey. Sydney Cockerell sent Q soon afterwards a copy of the

newly published satire, *Reunion All Round*, by the Rev. R. A. Knox, who was at the time a Fellow and Chaplain of Trinity College, Oxford. In his letter of thanks to the donor, Q said:

It's diabolically funny, and the great Jonathan himself might have signed it. But I reckon, knowing 'em, that the dons of Trin. Coll. Oxon. must be having a time with this young man, and I don't give him long to enjoy poking the Common Room fire with a sword.

I came down abruptly, having been summoned to lend my presence to a Fat Stock Show. (They didn't give me a prize)....

The harbour here is looking its best. I find our garden here full of roses and the other full of strawberries. I have written about half of a short play; started practising futurist verse (!) quite seriously, to find out how it is done—maybe I'll send you a specimen; and moreover have conscientiously corrected examination papers for the Mays.

A few weeks later the European war began. Bevil, who had been in the Officers' Training Corps at Oxford and had transferred to the Special Reserve in 1913, was immediately called up for service as a second lieutenant in the Royal Field Artillery. Before August was out he landed in France with the British Expeditionary Force.

CHAPTER VII

THE FIRST WORLD WAR (1914-18)

Q SPENT the rest of the summer in a very different way from what he had expected. He had been a leading member of the Territorial Force Association for Cornwall ever since its formation in 1908 and when the Territorials were mobilized on the outbreak of war he found himself fully occupied. His chief duty was to help recruiting, so that existing Territorial units in the county could be brought up to war-time strength and new units formed as quickly as possible. He helped in this work mainly by organizing and addressing public meetings and by writing.

His feelings and impressions during the early weeks of the war, together with some of his recruiting experiences, are faithfully recorded in his novel, *Nicky-Nan*, published in 1915. The hero of the book is a naval reservist of very straitened means who lives alone in part of the 'Old Doctor's' house at 'Polpier'—that is to say, in Jonathan Couch's house at Polperro—the rest of the house being occupied as a separate tenement by another naval reservist and his family. The scene is laid at 'Polpier' throughout the book, and the chief characters of the village are sketched with great sympathy.

Nicky-Nan is probably the least read of all Q's novels and he himself classed it with *Dead Man's Rock* and *The Blue Pavilions* as 'one of the bad uns'. It is true that it is hardly a novel in the ordinary sense of the word, since it has little plot. Yet it is an attractive and very human book and possesses historical value, for it records in admirable detail the effect of the outbreak of one of Europe's greatest wars on the life of an English village—the calling up and sending away of reservists; the rumours; the spy mania; the restlessness; the uncertainty; the anxiety; the recruiting meetings; the sending of anonymous letters and white feathers to supposed 'slackers' and cowards. It has 'dated' much less than one might expect, because it was dictated by its author's deep sympathy with his fellow men and particularly with the poor. It is far from deserving his strictures, for it gives a more faithful picture of English village life than any of his other writings.

Q's recruiting work kept him away from Cambridge, with the official approval of the University, for the earlier part of the autumn term. When he went back, he went alone: he and Lady Quiller-Couch had decided that it would be better for her and for their daughter to stay at Fowey until the war was over, owing to the prevailing uncertainty and the difficulties that would have to be faced in making the long journey between Fowey and Cambridge several times a year. The war lasted longer than was generally expected and by the time it was over they had grown accustomed to being apart during term. They also had to consider the question of expense. Q's income from his Professorship and his Fellowship combined did not at this time exceed £800 a year and never at any time exceeded £1300 plus free rooms in College and free dinner in Hall. This sum, even with the addition of the uncertain royalties from his books, was insufficient for him to maintain houses at both Cambridge and Fowey and continue to entertain all comers in the generous way for which he was celebrated. Since both he and his wife were too intensely attached to Fowey ever to think of leaving it, the result was that even when the war was over they never again took a house at Cambridge. Q continued to live a bachelor life in his rooms at Jesus College during term, he wrote home every day, and although he loved his terms at Cambridge he generally cut them as short as was decent. Ernest Harrison, the Registrary of the University, was inclined to think that in his later years he cut them even shorter than that; but the Registrary was not always an easy man to please.

When Q returned to Cambridge in the autumn of 1914 he found it very different from the place which he had left in the summer, for the great majority of the undergraduates had gone into the forces and a number of them had already been killed in action. At Jesus, which was typical of all the colleges, the undergraduates had filled the dining hall twice every evening before the war began. A single table could now accommodate them all. Q found the situation decidedly melancholy and he wrote:

We came up in October to find the streets desolate indeed. The good soldiers who had swarmed in upon town and college in August—a commander of cavalry occupied my rooms; too busy, I hope, to curse the dull contents of my shelves—had all departed for France. Nay, already many of them slept in French earth....

These had come and gone like a summer cloud: and October in Cambridge might have passed for the Long Vacation turned chilly. In the courts and around the Backs the gardeners were sweeping up the leaves, as ever; but no men passed on their way to lecture 'with the wind in their gowns'....In College one seldom met, never heard, an undergraduate. A few would gather in Hall, the most of them in their O.T.C. uniforms after a strenuous afternoon out by Madingley. The scholar read grace with an unwonted reverence: *Sic Deus in nobis et nos maneamus in illo*—and we took our seats to a meal decently frugal. As I looked down the hall, this one undergraduates' table reminded me of a road in the West Country I had followed a few days before, with the telegraph running beside it and on the wires the swallows gathering, discussing flight.

Q himself shared in the general restlessness and his lecturing suffered from it for a time. Soon after his return he gave two lectures on 'Patriotism in English Literature', and of these *The Cambridge Review* wrote:

The Professor seemed to us not quite at his best. He had many admirable things to say about the attitude to English literature adopted by German scholars and English examiners respectively; and we are convinced of the depraving influence which must be exerted by the Medieval and Modern Languages Tripos, Section A, when it stops its studies at 1832. But what is not clear is how otherwise the German view may be supposed to influence us, and what connection (for some connection seemed indicated) exists between their view of English literature, as something dead to be studied, and the spirit of Germanism which hastened the war. That Germany with her culture thinks it worth while to study English literature, though she do it under an illusion, is, on the face of it, a compliment. All this, however, will not at all deter us from going with the multitude to Sir Arthur Quiller-Couch's next lecture, nor from recognizing how living an influence he has brought to bear on the study of English literature in Cambridge.

Later in the term he gave a lecture on 'The Terms *Classical* and *Romantic*', which contained much sound common sense, expressed in such a way that his hearers and readers were never likely to forget it:

Gentlemen, I would I could persuade you to remember that you are English, and to go always for the thing, casting out of your vocabulary all such words as 'tendencies', 'influences', 'revivals', 'revolts'. 'Tendencies' did not write *The Canterbury Tales*; Geoffrey Chaucer wrote them. 'Influences' did not make *The Faerie Queene*; Edmund Spenser made it: as a man called Ben Jonson wrote *The Alchemist*, a man called Sheridan wrote *The Rivals*, a man called Meredith wrote *The Egoist*;

but he then disappointed many of his hearers by going off at a tangent to Germany and staying there for the rest of the lecture. This caused *The Cambridge Review* to say:

We shall really be rather glad if Sir Arthur Quiller-Couch will consent to take us back next term to the type of lecture which we enjoyed last year. Q on *Macbeth* was stimulating and admirable; Q on the terms 'classical' and 'romantic' finds it very hard to stick to the point. One can't help feeling that his lectures this term would have shown a very different complexion if they had been written without the disturbing influence of the war. Germany and the Germans have become a 'King Charles's head'; and we feel it may not be out of place to bring up against the Professor the 'golden saying of Marcus Aurelius' which he quoted in his first lecture: 'The best part of revenge is not to be like them.' If Germany may be considered to disparage our literature, which may be doubted, it is no good answer to disparage hers in return. One of the reasons why we hope the effects of the war will not become too penetrating is that we wish to hear more from Sir Arthur about the qualities of English, and less about the deficiencies of German literature and literary criticism.

Let it be frankly admitted that some passages in Q's war-time lectures were unworthy of him and would better have been left unprinted; but let it be remembered that he was enduring something that was probably outside the experience of his critic in *The Cambridge Review*—the daily and even hourly agony of wondering what was happening to his only son, who, practically from the beginning of the war to the end of it, was in the thick of the fighting against Germany.

Q managed to get through the autumn term somehow and then went home for Christmas but it was a melancholy Christmas for him, with his son absent for the first time in his life. When he returned to Cambridge early in 1915 he found it once more a changed place and he wrote in *The Cambridge Review*:

We returned in January to a vastly different Cambridge. She had become a garrison town....

The curfew no longer tolls the knell of parting day. It is not permitted. But when dusk has fallen and the Mayor and Corporation leave the world to darkness and to me, I walk in the Fellows' Garden, carefully hiding the ardent tip of my cigarette lest it should attract a Zeppelin.

There were now, he said, 'lines of artillery horses beside the Trumpington Road, Adams Road, Jesus Ditch', in which the horses stood fetlock deep in mud; there was mud on Midsummer Common and 'worse mud on the road to the Rifle Butts, where the M.A. warriors of the C.U.O.T.C. drill and improve their waists, though they may never serve their country'. Q himself, armed with a dummy rifle, drilled with 'the M.A. warriors', who were commanded by Sir Harry Stephen. They included such well-known senior members of the University as W. H. D. Rouse, the portly but gentle E. J. Rapson (Professor of Sanskrit), E. S. Prior (Professor of Fine Art), C. W. Previté-Orton, W. L. H. Duckworth, and R. C. Punnett (Professor of Genetics). These and other members of the detachment appeared in a parody of W. S. Gilbert, by 'Outsider', which *The Cambridge Review* published in its next issue after Q's reference to 'the M.A. warriors':

Dr Rouse.

When I first put this uniform on,
I said, as I looked in the glass:
'The dreaded occasion
Of England's invasion
Will surely not come to pass.
I look very well in these togs
And I think I could march to the Gogs.'
But alas! at the double
I got into trouble—
The roads have been turned into bogs;
Which I never counted upon
When I first put this uniform on.

Chorus of M.A.s.

The same thing occurred to me, too;
I thought I could march to the Gogs,
And I said: 'I have nothing to do
And my income has gone to the dogs.'

Professor Rapson.

When I *did* get this uniform on
I said to myself: 'I'm a toff;
But it's one to a hundred—
In fact, 'tis my one dread
I'll never get the damned things off.'

Chorus.

Ha! ha!
How they'd scoff
If he couldn't get the damned things off!

Rapson.

They declare I can't see my own belt.
Never mind! though unseen, it is felt.

Chorus.

O well done, Rapson,
To get all those straps on!...
(*Enter* Q)

Q.

> Good afternoon. A merry drill I wish you
> And recommend you the *Review's* last issue,
> Where I, in mentioning the muddy ruts
> Leading from Grange Road to the Rifle Butts,
> Made *butts* of *you*. I said you were no use:
> The only enemy you *might* 'reduce'
> Was your avoirdupois. Good afternoon.   (*Exit*)

Sir Harry Stephen.

> Up, dons, and at him ! (What's its name?) Platoon !
>   On, Gregory, Brindley, and Prior !
>   On, Sikes, and annihilate Q !
>   On, Foxwell and Previté,
>   Punish his levity,
> Make him *eat* the last *Cambridge Review* !...

Chorus.

> Come, Duckworth and Oldham and all,
> Punnett, Powles, Quiggin, answer the call !
>   For Q shall do homage
>   To Bushe-Fox and Bromwich—
> We're in for a fight after all.
>   Which *we* never counted upon
>   When we first put this uniform on.

From March to October 1915 Q was away from Cambridge on military duty in Cornwall—raising and equipping a pioneer battalion of the Duke of Cornwall's Light Infantry and putting it through its preliminary training. He held a temporary commission for the purpose, beginning as a lieutenant and being promoted to captain about three months later. In May, in the midst of his military duties, he had to set examination papers for the English section of the Medieval and Modern Languages Tripos and send them to Cambridge. The chairman of the examiners was the Rev. H. F. Stewart, at that time a Fellow of St John's College and afterwards of Trinity, and the correspondence that necessarily sprang up between them about the examination led to a life-long friendship. Dr Stewart found it necessary to rebuke Q for his delay in sending in his examination papers, which were urgently needed. In reply, Q wrote from Fowey on 21 May:

I am sorry indeed to have put you to such trouble: but in truth, as I conveyed in my telegram, we are almost desperately busy here, raising a new service battalion (D.C.L.I.): and on top of my share of recruiting for the battalion the War Office made me a temporary lieutenant to work up one company, and then declines to gazette and send down our officers to cope with the men pouring in. So I am left alone with the O.C. to wrestle with a thousand details of clothing contracts, army forms, billets, etc., besides taking parades and sitting on minor offences. What the O.C. will do on Monday I know not: for he is a stranger to the town. Sixty men were shot into us in a batch last Monday. I don't *suppose* they'll repeat this on Whit-Monday; but there's no knowing: and if they do, Heaven help us!

On 27 May he wrote to Dr Stewart again from Fowey:

Forgive a scrawl! I have been drilling and grilling for two hours in the eye of the sun: and if this letter is apparently blotted with a tear it has nothing to do with the Recording Angel and moreover it isn't a tear at all but perspiration.

I will post the General History and Shakespeare paper to-night. It is mostly ready and should be despatched with this: but I have to take the men on a six-mile route march after getting something to eat....

The War Office *won't* send officers: and my days for a week past have been 7.30 a.m.–1 a.m. The Colonel gets to bed at midnight and then I consider the History of English Literature 1780–1830. We are

> 1 colonel
> 1 lieutenant (myself)
> 1 sergeant-major
> 4 corporals
> 154 men

in this company. The other company has 180-odd men and is better officered. But I have to help officially in organizing that, too. We clothed 50 men on Tuesday, 38 yesterday, 18 to-day. So don't account me a rotter.

In spite of his heavy military work, he was still carrying out some at least of his civil duties. We find evidence of this in a letter written on 30 May, in which he says:

My poor wits were wandering when I concluded my last and also I was interrupted by a lady who wanted her child to be exempted from vaccination.

I think, though it doesn't concern you, that you will like to hear of a recruit who begged off parade on the ground that 'he wasn't took very well this morning'. Suffering from meiosis?

If the fellows weren't so amazingly tractable I don't know what we should do. They still look on me as an amiable eccentric when I examine their 160 chins every morning at 9.30. 'I never *belonged*, sir, to get shaved but on Saturday night.' But they are excellent fellows.

If the troops regarded him as an eccentric because of his insisting on their shaving every day they nevertheless had good reason to consider him an amiable one. Few military commanders, for instance, can have taken their men home to tea with them on their way back from a route march, as Q once took his whole company. Lady Quiller-Couch rose to the occasion and managed to feed them all. They sat at tables dotted about the lawn at The Haven and they ate the place bare. Even fewer military commanders can have been as paternal to their men as Q was on another occasion, when, after taking his company to bathe in the sea, he cut the toe-nails of a large number of them—'and they *were* toe-nails, too', he said some twenty years later.

On 7 June he wrote:

You will be glad to hear that we have raised two companies and have orders from the War Office to continue and push for a battalion. My own little lot are to-day 210 strong, and I took 'em a route-march this afternoon after a hard morning's drill;

and on 24 June:

My battalion, like the spirit of John Brown, is still marching along. To date:

> A Company, 224 men—complete.
> B Company, 224 men—complete,
> C Company, 100-odd,
> D Company, 40-odd,

all clothed and up to now, after great struggles with War Office forms, punctually fed and paid.

My boy continues to write cheerfully from France; and in the intervals of fighting collects large stores of cherries and gooseberries from deserted gardens in which the roses are smothering the holes made by shells.

He was back at Cambridge in October. During the academical year which began in that month he delivered a course of lectures afterwards published in book form as *Shakespeare's Workmanship*. Three of these, on *The Tempest*, were among the best lectures he ever gave. During this same academical year he devoted a great deal of thought to the future of English studies in the University and had a number of discussions with H. F. Stewart, who had already become a close friend and supporter, and with H. M. Chadwick, the Professor of Anglo-Saxon. The three were agreed that reforms were overdue. They wanted to see English recognized as a fully developed part of the University curriculum, with a Tripos of its own, instead of being merely a section of the Medieval and Modern Languages Tripos. They felt that the English syllabus needed widening and modernizing, that English should be more of a humane study than it had been, and that candidates should be able to sit for an examination in literature without being forced (as they then were) to be examined also in philology. Among those whom they consulted was Sir Walter Raleigh, the Cambridge man who had been Professor of English Literature at Oxford for some years. 'Some of his criticisms', Q wrote in January 1916, 'ought to help us a good deal: while one or two of the difficulties at which he boggles will (I believe) be solved *ambulando*.'

On 22 April 1916 Q's dramatized version of *The Mayor of Troy* was produced at the Haymarket Theatre, with Henry Ainley in the title role. Q had made various changes in the story: he had, for instance, given it a happy ending and changed the hero's name to Toogood. He wanted to call the play *It's Hard to be Toogood*, but Frederick Harrison, the producer, insisted on giving it the same title as the novel. A criticism of the play in *The Times*—unsigned, but known to be by Q's old colleague, A. B. Walkley—said: 'A

first play is apt to be like a first lecture, a first speech, a first
symphony. There are generally too many ideas, too many "movements" in it. Q's first play, to be sure, has one main idea or thesis,
but it has too many casual ideas, superfluous details, loose ends.
His main idea is the inconvenience caused all round by the return
of the dead to life [but] he fails to drive the idea home; he rather
fritters it away.' The audience was more pleased with the play than
Walkley and called for the author as well as the chief actors at the
end of the first performance. The times were, however, scarcely
propitious to new plays and *The Mayor of Troy* was taken off after
a run of three weeks. Q mentions some of the difficulties in the
way of its success in a letter which he wrote on 2 May:

> The stars in their courses have fought against my little play. Ainley
> was palsied with nervousness on the first night, and that let in the
> critics. Then a scene-shifter had a fit and died while setting Act 3. All
> the next week London had nightly warnings to stay at home because of
> Zeppelins, and the public fled to the country to enjoy safety and hot
> weather. Horrors on St Stephen's Green, Kut, crisis in Parliament—
> what is my little luck, to stand up against all that?
> But I'm not downcast. Patience, and shuffle the cards! The worst is
> that I am out of health; a fortnight of rehearsing, nine hours a day,
> knocked me up a bit.

In the autumn of 1916 he began the course of lectures which he
afterwards published as *The Art of Reading*. The proportion of
women to men in his audience was higher than ever, for the war
had drained the men's colleges to a very low ebb. At Jesus College
there were hardly more than a dozen undergraduates in residence
and the dons also were few in number. Several of them were
away on national service. Sydney Cockerell, who had been intimate with Q from the first, was no longer a Fellow of the college;
and Foakes-Jackson, who was an entertainment in himself, had
gone to be a Professor at New York, leaving Q the sole resident on
his staircase. As he was a man who loved the society of others and
responded very rapidly to his environment he found the term a
depressing one. He was further depressed by the fall of Mr
Asquith's ministry in December. All the time, too, he was

gnawed by anxiety for his son, who—except for a visit to England in April to receive the Military Cross from the King—had been in heavy fighting in France throughout the year. Bevil was home again on leave in December and Q refers to his visit in a letter that he wrote to Sydney Cockerell two days after Christmas:

I am recovering, or supposed to be recovering, from the $\phi\lambda\hat{v}$, and hardly feel well enough to care whether I do or don't. But I cheer up because my Boy has been home and imparted life to the whole situation. They have made him a major: which, as I told him, may make all the difference. . . .

I am low, sir—low. I foresee that, lacking you and Foakes-Jackson, I shall soon have to cut Jesus College and perhaps Cambridge. On top of which I foresee myself back in politics again and, in a corner of the world, wearing out a stupid end of life in politics, fighting a Cabinet of parvenus, prigs and Prussians. God! what an end to every hope of 1906!

I am writing lectures for next term. . . . I am—Heaven knows why it should be in this general defection of spirit—simply boiling over with plots of novels and plays, schemes of books, etc.

And I have this day sawn up about three cwt. of wood on my own farm, corrected about one-third of that weight of proofs, and dined sparsely but as a Christian. The carollers have been singing in the hall, and the holly and ivy make the usual background. Also it has been a heavenly December day—the sort of day, as A. J. Butler used to remark, God only serves out in short lengths. At 12.30 a.m. an air-ship (British) came swooping low over the house. As it rounded and turned westward again its side took the loveliest shine.

In his preface to *The Art of Reading* (which he dedicated to H. F. Stewart and H. M. Chadwick) Q says that the lectures contained in the book 'cover—and to some extent, by reflection, chronicle—a period during which a few friends, who had an idea and believed in it, were fighting to establish the present English Tripos at Cambridge'. The fight came to a head in the spring of 1917, after Q, Stewart and Chadwick had put their proposed reforms before their colleagues on the Special Board for Medieval and Modern Languages and had obtained their support. In February the Board made a report to the University, recommending that the Medieval and Modern Languages Tripos should be replaced by two Triposes. One of these was to be a Modern and Medieval Languages Tripos—the change of name was slight but significant—the other an English Tripos. Perhaps the most important part of the Board's proposals was that in the new Tripos the study of philology, of Anglo-Saxon, and of Middle English literature was to be optional and candidates could offer in their place Literary Criticism and Comparative Literature.

When the report was discussed by the Senate of the University in March it met with opposition. Dr Mayo naturally objected to both of the proposed new Triposes. According to the official account of the discussion he even went so far as to say that 'he did not hold him to be a genuine and patriotic Englishman who would not join him in the belief that it was impossible for an English university really to hold a genuine examination' in Modern and Medieval Languages. In order to get satisfactory examiners and lecturers, he said, the University would have to employ foreigners and thereby show that the Languages Tripos 'was not a genuine Cambridge study nor a genuine Cambridge examination'. In short, he maintained that 'the teaching of foreign languages was futile and was to be deprecated in the highest degree'. As for the proposed English Tripos, he need not do more than quote Plato, who said: 'I do not teach Hellenic to the Hellenes; the fact that they are born Hellenes precludes the necessity for Hellenising them; they are Hellenes all their lives.' Similarly, said Dr Mayo, an Englishman was English all his life and did not need to be taught English.

When Q replied to the criticisms of the report he said that it had been a grave scandal that, until as recently as three years before, Englishmen from English universities who wanted to learn their own language had had to go abroad to get what they wanted— even to Germany. There they were taught 'things which were often quite wrong, and even when right were taught in disproportion'. Cambridge, he said, wanted a chance to remove the scandal, just as Oxford had already removed it. Oxford and Cambridge ought not always to follow the same lines; but, if the report were adopted, he believed that 'they would produce a type of English scholar at Cambridge quite as accurate, quite as careful, as his brother at Oxford and not less humane'.

As a result of the discussion a few changes were made in the proposed syllabus of the English Tripos and a revised report was published at the beginning of May. The changes were slight and did nothing to satisfy the critics, who therefore continued their opposition. They were, however, defeated when a vote was taken in the Senate House on 19 May and thus the English Tripos was founded.

Opposition to the new Tripos was, nevertheless, still alive elsewhere. It came from the English Association and from other sources. 'Trouble is', Q wrote to Dr Stewart late in June, 'that everybody thinks he knows enough English to tender advice upon it. If this goes on, one of these days I'll buy a Slavonic dictionary, and a matchlock for Chadwick, and we'll raise trouble in the Balkans.' During the summer vacation he prepared a lecture, 'On a School of English', as 'a polite and reasoned statement of aims' in reply to the English Association's criticisms. He was also busy writing a new novel during the intervals between his numerous public engagements. His son, who had been home from France in June for 'a divine five days', was home again on short leave in September. Early in October he was wounded and Q wrote to Sydney Cockerell in reply to a letter of inquiry:

It was only a slight wound, I am thankful to say. A flying shard took him in the shoulder and cut him a bit. After having the wound dressed he resumed command and has not left his unit. He tried to keep it out of the lists; but the doctors have to report slight wounds (to protect themselves).

I hope to turn up on Tuesday and to lecture on Wednesday. 'Am just (this evening) back from the north coast here, where for a few days I have been trying to get my nerves right after finishing a novel.

Q's 'polite and reasoned statement of aims' was delivered at Cambridge on 17 October and was well summed up in *The Cambridge Review* by an anonymous writer, who said:

Sir Arthur Quiller-Couch's lecture may fairly be regarded as a Second Inaugural. Things have changed since he first spoke to us, five years ago. To-day, thanks to the English Tripos, the Professor of English Literature stands on a new level and surveys a different prospect. Beyond a quiet note of triumph, there was nothing unexpected in Sir Arthur's utterance. Now, as always, he is in arms against professionalism in literature; now, as always, he confesses three articles of belief (1) that Literature cannot be divorced from life, (2) that Literature cannot be understood apart from the men who have made it, (3) that Literature is a living art, to be practised as well as admired.

These tenets were richly illustrated by pieces of literature, and its reverse, from the Authorized Version to F. A. Paley—all admirably read, in spite of the bad light in the Lecture Room—and by many phrases which expressed the speaker's own conviction and which will stick in the minds of his hearers. We content ourselves with quoting one:

'All thoughts, as well as all passions, all delights—*votum, timor, ira, voluptas*—whatsoever, in short, engages man's activity of soul or body, may be deemed the subject of literature, and is transformed into literature by process of recording it in memorable speech.'

There could surely be no better motto for the new enterprise. We wish the ship, thus fairly launched, calm seas and a prosperous voyage.

The novel that Q finished writing in the autumn of 1917 was *Foe-Farrell*, published in the following year. This 'Jekyll-and-Hyde kind of story', as Q himself called it, is dedicated 'To anyone who supposes that he has a worse enemy than himself'. Its heroes are John Foe, a scientist, who has experimented for some years on the passions of animals, and Peter Farrell, a prosperous business man of little education. Farrell believes (wrongly) that Foe is practising vivisection and stirs up public opinion against him. As a result, Foe's laboratory is attacked and plundered by a mob and the carefully compiled records of all his experiments are destroyed. Foe thereupon conceives an undying hatred for Farrell and tells him that he will pursue him wherever he goes and finally kill him. He follows Farrell all round England, to the South of France, to the United States, to Peru and on board a ship bound for Australia. The ship is wrecked on the voyage and Foe and Farrell are the only two who survive to reach a Pacific island. After some time Foe gets away on a schooner, deliberately leaving Farrell to his fate.

Farrell gets away later and now becomes the implacable enemy and hunter of Foe, whom he reduces to rags. Foe finally murders Farrell and when he looks close into the face of his dead enemy he is horrified to see that it is just like his own. 'I swear to God', he says, 'it was not Farrell's face but my own I stared into.' A juror at the inquest, which Foe attends voluntarily, notices the same thing and faints. The coroner returns an open verdict. Foe writes to a friend to say that he is going to commit suicide. The two men have exchanged natures during the story—and that explains the hyphen in the title. As Q put it, when Foe in the end kills Farrell 'he actually kills himself—he kills the man he himself was before the feud started'.

In the Epilogue, the man who has told the story of Foe and Farrell to his comrades in a French dug-out during the war of 1914-18 is asked the moral of it all. 'I can give you *that* all right', he answers, 'and if you have any use for it you may apply it to this blasted war. As I see it, the more you beat Fritz by becoming like him, the more he has won. You may ride through his gates under an Arch of Triumph; but if he or his ghost sits on your saddle-bow, what's the use? You have demeaned yourself to him; you cannot shake him off, for his claws hook in you, and through the farther gate of Judgment you ride on, inseparables condemned.'

The moral is epitomized in the maxim of Marcus Aurelius that Q prefixed to the book as a motto: 'The best kind of revenge is not to become like him.' Some have imagined that Q was prompted to write *Foe-Farrell* by a feeling of remorse for his remarks about the Germans earlier in the war; but that cannot have been so, because he started to write the book during the spring of 1913 at latest. Its theme, moreover, had long fascinated him. We find it occupying a corner of *Nicky-Nan* and *News from the Duchy*. In *Lady Good-for-Nothing* (1910) Q remarks that 'Our enemies in this world are dearer to us than friends. They cling closer'; and in *Old Fires and Profitable Ghosts*, published in 1900, one of the stories, 'The Room of Mirrors', is *Foe-Farrell* in embryo. He returned to the same theme in conversation and in his letters during the war of 1939-45, when the British Government ordered German prisoners to be put in chains in retaliation for the chaining of British prisoners by the Germans.

Foe-Farrell was Q's last completed novel and is one of his best. Although it is a story with a moral, the moral does not obtrude and the story holds the reader from beginning to end. It was written, Q said, 'in counterpoint all the way through'; but the critics, with one exception, 'all missed guessing that when a story-teller of some experience lays all his cards on the table in that apparently artless way he may be intending to test the clever while satisfying the simple'.

At the beginning of 1918 the war looked as if it might go on for years. 'Few of us', Q wrote afterwards, 'felt able to hope that our then deserted colleges would fill again in our time; some of us prophesied an end for ourselves of sad retirement in the shade of libraries.' Apart from a handful of men invalided out of the forces or rejected as medically unfit, his lecture audiences consisted entirely of women. Food, other than the bare essentials, was becoming difficult to get and women spent a good deal of their time standing in queues outside shops.

Consequently, when Q was announced to preach at St Edward's Church one Sunday morning in January and the women crowded to hear him, *The Cambridge Review* remarked:

> Ah me! what Habit makes poor women do!—
> Queue every weekday, and on Sunday Q.

During the next few years he occupied the pulpit at least four times at St Edward's and once at least at All Saints' Church, just opposite the gate of Jesus College, and drew large congregations. An undergraduate newspaper, *The Old Cambridge*, said in 1922: 'Sir Arthur Quiller-Couch is preaching at St Edward's Church to-morrow morning. An ordinary service will take place in the evening.' It must be confessed, however, that although he was an extraordinarily good lecturer he was no preacher. Preaching was not in his line: he would never have preached at all but for the importunity of one or two clerics among his acquaintances. He was a loyal Anglican all his life; but he had no 'message' and was deficient in theological equipment and (despite the claims of Brother Copas to the contrary) in knowledge of church history.

During the spring and summer terms of 1918 he continued with his lectures on 'The Art of Reading' and with his Aristotle classes. In the summer vacation he organized bands of schoolboys and others, male and female, to help with the harvest in his part of Cornwall. In September Bevil was home again on leave from France and Q wrote afterwards:

We've had a heavenly time. It wound up with our sailing him up the river here seven miles to Lostwithiel station and seeing him and his sister off to a two days' riot of shopping and theatre-going. Then his mother and I pulled home on the ebb in the dusk of a lovely evening: but it was very much on the ebb and very much in the dusk.

Mothers are wonderful. But to-morrow we are off for a small holiday: Bath, Malvern, Broadway, Warwick, Oxford and home: that appears to be the programme.

When he returned to Cambridge in October he gave the two final lectures of his course on 'The Art of Reading'. In the second of them, delivered on 6 November, he was able to describe the war as 'now happily on the point of a victorious conclusion'. It ended on the 11th, at eleven o'clock in the morning. Five years later, when Q was delivering an address at All Saints' Church, he recalled vividly his feelings on the first Armistice Day. He remembered, he said,

a jolly man rushing into a shop and shouting to the wife of it that the guns had ceased fire and she could stop fretting about her man. (He himself, he explained to me, fraternizing, had—in his own words— 'known what it was with the Bulgarians'.) Well—the awful strain was over at last: and to one who for four years and more had endured it, here was, not only the salvation of his country achieved at length, but release from the awful dragging anxiety for his own, the hideous terror of any telegraph boy walking towards his house....

Do you, residents of Cambridge, remember that day? Do you remember the heedless rowdy crowd in your market, and the lorries parading in the silent rain?

Well, I am not saying a word against that. Youth will have its revulsion. Youth won the war, and (God knows) youth deserved any and every jolly revulsion of feeling. As for us others, the strain had been too long, and anyhow we had not deserved as youth had. So— I am going to be quite frank with you, my hearers—if actual Armistice Day in 1918 turned for some of us to an afternoon and evening of dreariness, settling down to a black depression and foreboding, attribute it for the moment to nothing worse than that, for us, loving our sons, the strain had been too long.

CHAPTER VIII

THE AFTERMATH OF THE WAR (1918–23)

EXCEPT for the slight wound that he had received in 1917 Bevil Quiller-Couch had come through the war unscathed. As soon as the fighting was over he moved forward into Germany with his battery, which was to form part of the army of occupation. He could have been demobilized almost at once if he had wished, but he wrote to his parents to say that he preferred to wait until the men under his command, and their horses, were free to return to England for demobilization in a body. During the winter he came home for a period of leave and while he was in England he announced his engagement to a daughter of his father's old friend, Charles Cannan. The wedding was fixed for June and a congenial post with a shipping company was waiting for him as soon as he was demobilized, so that his future looked rosy. After visiting his fiancée at Oxford he rejoined his battery at Duren.

On the evening of 6 February 1919, when Q was at Cambridge, he received a telegram to say that his son was dangerously ill. Next morning, by the first train, he left for Fowey. He arrived home late that evening, just in time to prevent his wife from being the first to learn from another telegram that Bevil was dead. He had died of pneumonia on the morning of the 6th, after a short illness. Q returned at once to London and met his son's fiancée. They went to the War Office together to try to get permission to go to Germany for the funeral, but were unsuccessful.

Q then returned to Fowey. He had been completely stunned at first by the tragedy that had befallen him; but now that he had time to think about the loss of the son to whom he had been so profoundly attached he suffered great agony. Even so, he speedily remembered that his wife's loss was as great as his own, if not greater, and he seriously thought of resigning his Professorship, so that he could be with her all the time. 'My time at Cambridge is not likely to be long', he wrote to a pupil; 'the household is so badly broken up that my duty seems to lie at home. I shall be sorry indeed to leave Cambridge: but there it is.' He changed his mind about leaving Cambridge, however, and tried to get relief from his pain by undertaking more and yet more work. After a year of this he wrote to a friend:

I have been rather heavily overworking—at Cambridge and, later, at Oxford—on examination work. It deadens pain. But I begin to see that it were better—and braver—to face the pain and 'have it out': for by shirking it one's whole mind gets deadened. Really I don't care, half my time, what happens in a world that has killed my dearest and most natural hope.

He was a determined man and he put this resolution into effect. From that time onward, although his son's image never became blurred in his memory, he faced the future with great courage and turned with renewed application to his literary work, his academical work at Cambridge, his public work in Cornwall, and his social activities.

In 1920, at the invitation of the veteran publisher, J. M. Dent, he became general editor of a new series of English texts for use in schools. They were called *The King's Treasuries of Literature* and were to do for children, Mr Dent said, what his Everyman's Library had done for adults. The venture was highly successful. During Q's lifetime over 250 volumes were published and there can hardly have been a school in the kingdom in which *The King's Treasuries* were unknown. Their great success was no doubt partly due to a feature that was unusual at the time in school books— their attractive bindings, in which Q's taste for bright colours was very evident. Another invitation that he accepted about the same time came from A. R. Waller, Secretary of the Cambridge University Press, who asked him to edit Shakespeare's plays in collaboration with Professor Dover Wilson. The fourteen comedies, each with an Introduction by Q, began to appear in 1921 and were completed in ten years. After that, Professor Dover Wilson continued the editing alone.

Q's interest in Shakespeare was perhaps at its keenest about this time and early in 1921 he took a leading part in forming a Cambridge branch of the British Empire Shakespeare Society. He became president of the branch and the Master of Jesus College became treasurer. The object of the Society was 'to promote greater familiarity with Shakespeare, particularly from the point of view of dramatic representation, and to demonstrate that although our great master has been given the first place in the Study he wrote primarily for the Stage, and that in order to be realized he must be visualized'. The branch normally met in the Master's Lodge at Jesus College and passed the evening reading Shakespeare's plays aloud. Q often took part in the reading, as also did the Master of Jesus. On special occasions the Society gave public readings in the Guildhall and once each summer they performed a play in the Master's garden, with the venerable walls of the college chapel as a background, or (if it was wet) in the A.D.C. theatre.

Q had already accepted the presidency of the recently founded Village Drama Society. He held the office for eight years and during his vacations addressed meetings of the Society in various parts of England. His remarks were frequently directed to curbing the well-meant activities of some of the better educated members of the Society. These would-be reformers were anxious to make village players abandon the use of their local dialects in favour of standard English and tried to force their own selection of plays on the performers in preference to the melodramas that they loved. Q reminded them that Theocritus, Homer, Sappho, Burns and Bunyan wrote in dialect; that the average village is self-centred and lives its own life; and that drama must consequently be presented to it as its own life and not (for instance) as in the medieval Nativity plays that the educated were so fond of thrusting on village players. He pointed out that plain village people have a reason for greatly preferring melodrama to high-class tragedy. 'Melodrama', he said, 'is based on poetic justice. Every week, and often twice a week, village people are taught that vice is punished and virtue rewarded, and that the inequalities of this world are put right in the next. It is not surprising, then, that for once they should like to see them put right in this world.'

Since Q never possessed a car, his numerous public engagements and his regular journeys between Cambridge and Fowey forced him to spend many hours every year in trains or waiting for trains. During the years that immediately followed the war he devoted these hours to the preparation of a new anthology, about which he wrote to H. F. Stewart:

If, in your reading, you happen to spot any passages of really good prose, it would be a favour to have note of 'em. I am up to the waist (and have been for some time) in an *Oxford Book of English Prose*— a by-product of which employ is that one gets various and entirely undeserved reputations by perusing in railway carriages such works as Law's *Serious Call* or *The Rights of Man*.

The marvel of the world to me is how so many men get through so much reading. I *have* read the Bible at the stretch of a chapter a day for some years, side by side with the Revised Version: have ploughed through two or three authors just as religiously; but am always a snail.

Grim reflection! there was poor old Methuselah with nothing to read; and here's you and me, dear Christian brother, with no time to read even the Fathers—the constant perusal of whom I've just found recommended to me in a spirited sermon by Bishop Hall.

Q was certainly working very hard at this time, for when the war of 1914–18 ended there was a great increase in the number of undergraduates at Cambridge and many of the newcomers were attracted to the English Tripos, the first examination for which was held in 1919. The class list that year was a short one, but it grew annually and in 1920 and 1921 contained the names of several who afterwards became well known as authors or critics—G. B. Harrison, J. B. Priestley, Gerald Bullett, F. R. Leavis, Basil Willey, Frank Kendon and Rosamond Lehmann. The increase in the size of the University was partly due to the influx of men and women whose education had been interrupted or delayed by the war, but even when these had gone out of residence the University remained considerably larger than it had ever been before 1914. At the end of the Lent term of 1920 Q wrote:

I am just off to Cornwall, pretty well beaten to a rag with this term's work. We have some 160 men and women reading for the English Tripos at this moment: and the colleges *must* find people to take their essays: for I simply cannot go on feeding the creatures who howl all day long on this doorstep. Save for one walk down to the towpath on the first day of the Lents, I haven't had an hour's exercise since I came up in January.

In the preface to a further volume of his lectures that was published two years later he wrote:

None of us, I will swear, anticipated what was to come upon us, as it were in a tidal wave—the amazing, portentous refluence of youth into the universities.

It came; and it was such that we could scarcely have coped with it, even if prepared. I for one, at any rate, had to revert to the old method of familiar discourse if the hungry generations were not to tread me down. I must offer my apologies to the reader for the result, but my thanks to Heaven for the cause.

Q was already planning to reform the English Tripos by dividing it into two Parts. In the summer of 1922 he wrote:

What I'm groping after is a second Part of the Tripos which shall (1) mainly concern itself with English *thought*, and (2) be a stiff test of our men's capacity to *write* (which includes thinking). What we want is a Part II that will turn out men provided with some useful principles for statesmanship, the better journalism, etc., and some knowledge of what Englishmen have thought from time to time. For my part, I believe that nowadays the true mission of the English Tripos is to preach the spirit of Greece.

The Tripos was divided in 1928. Two or three years later Q wrote to Mr Stanley Baldwin (afterwards Lord Baldwin of Bewdley), who had recently been elected Chancellor of the University: 'The English Tripos is now well on its legs—two legs, which is funny for a "tripos". They are called Part I and Part II: and both are solid. When I came up, there were some eighteen or so reading for a narrow little school. We have now some 140–150 *annually* taking a really noble Tripos.'

Q's lectures continued to attract as big crowds as ever when the war was over. The Girton and Newnham contingents, arriving early at the lecture theatre, packed the seats, leaving little more than standing room for the men; and in May 1920 *The Granta* published a topical parody of Alfred Noyes's poem, *Go down to Kew in Lilac Time:*

A Song for a May Morning, sung by the Ladies of Girnham.

Go down to Q in lilac time, in lilac time, in lilac time,
Go down to Q in lilac time, it isn't far from Girnham;
And you shall listen in a row to eloquence divinely slow;
Go down to Q in lilac time, it isn't far from Girnham.

Late arrivals stand in gloom and fret and fume, and fret and fume;
But there they say, and they should know, fresh flowers of rhetoric
    do grow
And sweetly bloom and sweeter blow (unconscious quite of Girnham).

So rise up early, put on speed, and sit and read, and sit and read;
And if you're aged and infirm it's never more than thrice a term;
So come in thousands, squeeze and squirm with all the fair of Girnham.

Of fiery Shelley is his lay (or was the day 'fore yesterday),
And Shelley's skylark, envying him, was far too bored to soar and skim,
For there were none to hear her hymn in all the fields of Girnham.

Come down to Q in lilac time, in lilac time, in lilac time,
Come down to Q in lilac time, it isn't far from Girnham;
And you shall listen in a row to eloquence divinely slow
(It has to last an hour, you know), so come along from Girnham.

In the autumn of the same year another undergraduate journal, *The Old Cambridge*, published a humorous exaggeration of the scene outside the Arts School on the mornings when Q was announced to lecture:

Remarkable scenes were witnessed outside the Arts School at a quarter to twelve on Wednesday morning. Long before that hour, a stranger to Cambridge might have been astonished at the sight of mixed crowds thronging their way to that narrow thoroughfare to which the Bath

Hotel lends a touch of old romance. Across the Market Place, down Peas Hill they came, like rats in the wake of the Pied Piper.

Mounted police guarded the iron gates of the Arts School to allow a free passage to those returning from Mr Malthus's lecture on 'Bimetallism'. Their efforts were successful until a little before twelve o'clock, the hour appointed for the English Professor's address on Shelley. Then with sudden ferocity the crowd made a combined attack upon the deserted pavements of the courtyard. In the frenzied rush women screamed and the younger children howled. The contingent of police slowly receded, contesting every inch of the ground. The more exasperated section of the crowd began to claw up the red pebbles of the courtyard and wrest the railings from their sockets.

At this point the temper of the mob became exceedingly dangerous and woeful consequences might have ensued but for the timely arrival of a stalwart official of the School. Rapidly descending the few steps he held aloft a fluttering sheet of paper: there was tidings in his mouth. A hush fell on the expectant multitude; and St Mary's began to strike twelve. This was the signal for the withdrawal of the police, who had faithfully done their duty.

The official's voice was like one crying in the wilderness: 'The English Professor's lecture is, as usual, postponed until next week.'

A tense moment supervened. The women gripped their handlebars; the men, at a sharp word of command, ordered railings; and as from one voice the cry went up to an impassive heaven, drowning the last peals from the belfry: 'We want Q! We want Q!' But his place was nowhere to be found. The crowd soberly dispersed, the men to their studies, the women to their dressing-tables.

Our Own Correspondent from Fowey writes: 'A little before twelve this morning I was walking along the cliff above the harbour and was pleased to meet the author whose novels have sung so faithfully the praises of Cornwall. In one hand he carried a copy of *The Tempest*; in the other a page of manuscript, but he was intent on neither. I have now to note a strange occurrence, and to give credence to my story I am able to specify the hour. Fowey Church was striking noon when Sir Arthur dropped his manuscript and, inexplicably placing one hand to his ear, began to sing that famous ditty: *I hear you calling me*. His top note was more pure than Caruso's. On the last stroke of twelve he passed on, musing. I was glad to retrieve the discarded document. It was headed: *Shelley: A Lecture to be delivered in the University of Cambridge*, *in all probability during the October Term*, 1921. There followed one word only: "Gentlemen".'

A few of those who attended Q's lectures perhaps did so because that was the fashionable thing to do, but he was unnecessarily sensitive when he wrote to H. F. Stewart in 1922:

I seem to read signs in Cambridge that I'd better shut up *public* lectures for a bit. The *Old Cambridge*, this last term, started suggesting that they were a silly 'fetish'. But there's no honour in that discovery. I made it myself, years ago. It seems to me that (with a little money in hand) I can now hire a few 'spot' lecturers and confine my voice for a while to *Poetics* and other classes in the Divinity Schools. Think this over; and, as you would help, tell yourself that Q doesn't want these audiences. He *does* want, weakly or not, to be remembered for a hand in making the English Tripos.

Meanwhile, he was receiving many pressing invitations to lecture away from Cambridge, and in the autumn of the same year he wrote:

I didn't write on Sunday, having to catch up with all kinds of fool correspondence which I'd neglected all the week for apple-gathering— a far more engaging job than telling people I cannot and will not lecture at West Ham, Kettering, Tonbridge, Hull, Manchester; no, nor at Glasgow, Aberdeen, Dumfries, St Andrews, nor yet in Edinburgh. This ridiculous demand does really and truly vex me. All my life I've been writing stuff which I've tried to make sound, and people won't read it: and then all of a sudden I get this reputation which I feel to be largely a fraud. Well, the comfort is, *I've* done precious little to encourage it. You mustn't take this for mock-modest. I *do* feel that I'm earning my salary at Cambridge. Otherwise I should have left long before this. But it is being earned at my *classes*, or in private talk with the young on C. Staircase, Jesus College.

It was about this time that he declined an invitation to lecture in the United States, his reason (or one of his reasons) being that he would not travel in a Prohibitionist country; but he did not visit America even when Prohibition was abolished. The Scilly Isles remained his farthest point west, Biarritz his farthest south and Genoa his farthest east.

The return of peace brought with it the revival of numerous University clubs and societies that had lain dormant throughout the war. Among them were the Cambridge University Cruising Club, of which Q was president from 1919 to his death, and two dining clubs to which he belonged, known as Ad Eundem and The Society. The Cruising Club was composed mostly of undergraduates, the dining clubs were confined to seniors. Ad Eundem had been founded in 1865 and met alternately at Oxford and Cambridge, from each of which it drew half of its twenty-eight members. Normally, half the members were residents, the other half non-residents. Q had been elected a non-resident member of the Oxford side in 1897 but had resigned in 1903. He was elected a member of the Cambridge side in 1920. The other Cambridge members at the time included Henry Jackson, Francis Jenkinson (the University Librarian), Augustine Birrell, Baron von Hügel and Sir Horace Darwin. Those who were elected later during Q's time included Stanley Baldwin, G. M. Trevelyan, and Lord Birdwood (Master of Peterhouse).

The Society consisted entirely of Cambridge men and normally met twice a term, the members taking turns at being hosts. In Q's time it included some of those who belonged to Ad Eundem and also Peter Giles (Master of Emmanuel), H. H. Brindley, Sir Stephen Gaselee, H. F. Stewart, A. B. Ramsay (Master of Magdalene), H. R. Dean (Master of Trinity Hall), J. T. Sheppard (Provost of King's), Louis Clarke (Director of the Fitzwilliam Museum), Sir Herbert Richmond (Master of Downing), and Sir Charles Darwin (Master of Christ's). Q was in his element at the meetings of both these clubs and whenever he was to be host he devoted careful attention to the menu. In October 1922 he wrote:

The Society dined with Peter Giles on Monday last, and it was not a dinner of herbs. I drank largely but judiciously and awoke with a clean tongue and in charity with the world. I am to be host on November 20th and am preparing a Spanish ham 'with trimmings'. You boil it slowly in Chablis, and the intelligent animal tells you when it is cooked to perfection by quietly turning upside down. And yet people question the intelligence of our dumb companions.

The revival of the University after the war was accompanied by the return of many dons who had been away on national service and by the arrival of new ones. The two sets of rooms on the floor above Q that Foakes-Jackson had monopolized until his departure to America now had two different tenants. One of these was W. H. Duke, whose all too early death a few years later robbed the University of a sensitive classical scholar and of one of the most gentle and humane of all its members. The other was Alexander Nairne, who had succeeded Foakes-Jackson as Dean of the College.

Nairne was a man with a great mind but was of small stature. What little there was of him was mostly skin and bone and the hard Cambridge winters were a great trial to him. His quaint ways were a frequent source of amusement to Q, who nevertheless had a great affection and respect for him. Nairne, for his part, was very fond of Q and read nearly everything that he ever wrote. Like Q, he enjoyed good company and knew how to order a meal; but, being an ascetic, he hardly touched the carefully chosen fare that he provided for his guests, his own usual meal being a stale bun and a cup of coffee. After some years of utterly ignoring current affairs he decided that it was his duty to take an interest in them and he persuaded Q (much against his will) to let him share his newspaper. For a time he was astonished and interested in his discovery of what was going on in the world around him, almost as much as if he came from another planet, but he soon began to lose interest. In politics he generally leaned to the Left and more than once worked for the Labour Party during elections. He nevertheless accepted the office of president of a small society known as the Royal Martyr Church Union, which venerated Charles I as a saint. To judge from this society's publications, its members were mainly High Tory if not Jacobite in politics and could hardly hear Cromwell's name mentioned without spitting. When they heard that Nairne was going to read a paper to them about the Royal Martyr they were delighted and arrived in large numbers to hear it. Their delight turned to disappointment and annoyance when he delivered a discourse of which the theme was that if there *was* a greater and a better man than Charles I in the seventeenth century it was Cromwell, and that if only these two wonderful men could have met regularly to discuss affairs of State all would have been well.

Both Q and Nairne were much attached to Thomas Okey, the first Professor of Italian at Cambridge, who was elected in 1919, when he also became a Fellow of Caius College. 'Okey is a daisy', Q used to say. Anyone who saw the three men for the first time might well have taken Q for a sea captain, Nairne for what he was —a scholar and an ascetic—and Okey for a leisured aristocrat. In fact, Okey was the son and grandson of East End basket-makers, and had himself been a basket-maker for many years. From the time when he left an elementary school at the age of eleven he had had no education except what he managed to give himself while working at his trade. When, to his great astonishment, he was elected to the chair of Italian at Cambridge he was terrified at the prospect of lecturing to a University audience. He nearly wrote to the Vice-Chancellor to say that he declined the office, but was reassured by a letter from Q, whom at the time he had never met. Okey never forgot this kindness. Not long before he died he made waste-paper baskets as presents for Q and Nairne; and in the course of a letter about the baskets written to a friend he said:

Q always hated lecturing and I often heard him exclaim in the Arts School, where we met before our turns came, 'Okey! why do we do it? Why *do* we do it?' in the most tragic voice, as though about to be executed...Q [was] the best friend to hold out a helping hand to me, a poor nervous timid creature among so many *un*human creatures (as they seemed)—the first to hold out a human hand of welcome and to give me heart and courage. I shall never forget the letter he wrote to me out of pure helpfulness. It was a precious gift and a rare endowment to me an utter stranger.

During his vacations Q was as busy as he had ever been with Cornish affairs. In the summer of 1919, when the international treaties had been signed and the official peace celebrations held, he was asked to draw up an appropriate resolution for the County Council of Cornwall. This he did; and when the resolution had been passed it was cut into the wall of the County Hall at Truro:

That this Council, the members all rising and standing in their places, do thank and adore Almighty God for His merciful goodness in delivering our nation forth from the late protracted war: for sustenance through toil and fear, agonies and most instant perils: for the issue awarded upon His eternal judgement: and for the restored blessings of peace.

That this Council do furthermore record its gratitude to one and all of Cornwall who in their several estates have come forward to help and protect the realm either by arms or with counsel; and in special do commend to the remembrance of their countrymen and commit to the tenderness of God all those who by payment of their lives have redeemed their country, that its life might be perpetuated and its honour increased by their honour.

And lastly that all members of the Council do resolve unite and agree in prayer: that in all matters entrusted to its province their hearts may be ruled and their counsels singly directed to the better establishment of God's kingdom on earth under peace and goodwill towards men.

Q was still vice-chairman of the County Education Committee and much more even than a vice-chairman's share of work fell to him, for the chairman, R. G. Rows, was now over eighty and almost blind. Big schemes of educational reconstruction and expansion were in hand at the time, but Q managed to cope with them and also with his magisterial and other public duties. His private correspondence at the time shows how fully he was occupied. In July 1922, for instance, he wrote:

All the back-end of the week is filled up with the sort of committee work (local) that makes up an alleged vacation. All yesterday I spent at Truro on a School Building and Furnishing Committee. This morning I spent on agenda of full Education Committee, at which I must take the chair to-morrow: and this very afternoon I've (1) presided at

Harbour Commission, and (2) attended meeting for winding up accounts of local War Memorial.

> Two children in two neighbouring villages,
> The one but just allowed to wash himself,
> The other scarcely given time for *that*—
> So runs the round of life from hour to hour.
>
> (Copyright)

Later in the same month he wrote:

I am a bad man, not to have written before. But I think I warned you that dull business was taking me to Oxford and London: and on my return I had to run in double harness (*a*) a sweating conclusion of *Much Ado* and (*b*) some work for Exeter University College and (*c*) finally there overtook me yesterday the fearful job of pounding through reports and getting up a brief to carry our Education Committee through County Council to-day. It went off all right, but I reached my happy home to-night feeling like a wrung rag.

I stayed with Bridges at Oxford. He asserts that the view from his garden overlooking Oxford beats the view from Fiesole. Well, I don't know about that: but it is assuredly mighty fine. We bumped into Oxford next morning and elected Gordon to be successor to Raleigh: and then I lunched in Merton.... toddled aside into my old college and its beloved but rather battered lime-walk and steered for London. Spent the evening after dinner on a perch on Barrie's roof in the Adelphi —finest night view of London—and next day met Peter Giles at Queensland House in the Strand, passed a pleasant Oxford youth for a post at Brisbane and caught the 2 p.m. ex-Paddington for home: and found the evening view from this garden, after all, not inferior to Bridges' 'dreaming spires' or Barrie's lights of London.

A week later he wrote:

No man can tell, in these parts, what he won't suffer from visitors in August (and they all pour in just as if life here was a perpetual holiday, and would all feel so dreadfully hurt if we didn't mix cider-cups and put up luncheon-baskets and sail down the bay and tell where to search for couries or, like Caliban, get 'em ' young scamels from the rocks'. And they multiply and bring their children, and 'it's always so jolly'—whereas it's wae-wae! for me to be led out to play in these haunted spots—these very brach-pools). But there's work. Dover

Wilson comes to-morrow to spend three days slogging through text of *Love's Labour's Lost* and mapping out my Introduction to that *most* difficult play—concerning which, as yet, I only know that nobody has ever put up a rational explanation of it. Such arrant rot interspersed with passages so lovely!...

I spent Monday making magistrates, on Advisory Committee. Life is a mixed bag. We are seven—in classical phrase—on that Committee down here and the freak of it is that the Labour representative is the most anxious of us 'not to lower the status of the Bench'.

Towards the end of August he was always very busy organizing the annual regatta at Fowey. In a letter written to H. F. Stewart on 27 August 1922, his light-hearted comments on the near approach of the regatta are interrupted by a brief outburst of the sorrow that he generally managed to conceal:

This house is much exposed to guests and visitors just now, and more-over Regatta week is upon us. Didn't know that I was a Commodore, didn't you? Marry, yes: and one that hath two gowns and everything handsome about him—though they do say that the Cambridge one is the more becoming. Time was when I used to enjoy this sort of thing—firing guns and starting yacht races; and once on a day I, being laden and accoutred with two guns, stop-watch, megaphone, cartridge bag and what-not, was asked by a very rich man at the Club landing-steps, 'Do you really enjoy this sort of thing?' 'Well', says I, 'now you speak of it, I suppose I do, in a simple way.' 'Then you're a lucky fellow', says he, 'for I've been chasing pleasure these forty years and haven't caught up with it yet.'

There's a sequel. That man made a good end. His yacht foundered in the Bay of Biscay, and all took to the boats, in bitter weather, and made the land somehow. But he was dead, frozen stiff, when they lifted him out, having shed his oilskin coat to wrap up his small child. He was the lucky fellow after all. He could save his boy.

So I don't much enjoy starting yacht-races nowadays; but, as Aristotle has doubtless observed somewhere (but as the newspaper correspondents put it, 'I am writing away from my books in a remote corner of Cornwall and cannot supply the exact reference') unless somebody, firing a gun, provides an immediate cause, we must relegate yacht-racing to the category of τὰ ἄμορφα, having neither beginning nor end,

Q as Commodore of the Royal Fowey Yacht Club

nor any recognizable middle, and things of that sort go on to infinity being offensive.

On top of regattas I am much pestered by young men who think they are good enough to be Professors of English Literature at the University of Leeds and want me to write testimonials for them. Can you tell me (who never, to my recollection, received one) if in this matter of testimonials it really *is* better to give than to receive? Giving em is so damnable that I can hardly imagine it better than *anything*.

A week later he sent an account of the regatta to the same correspondent:

The regatta went off in grand weather—and the sea like champagne—such a γέλασμα, and *O litus vita mihi dulcius*, etc.; and, what's more to the point, I got away fifteen boats in one of the prettiest starts ever seen. After which my wife and I received the rank and fashion on the Club terrace to the strains of the Royal Marines—who played with extreme virtuosity through a programme of the world's very worst music. As Hamlet observes somewhere, 'What a piece of work is a military band! In form and moving how express and admirable! How infinite in percussion! Instead of which it goes about playing *Love's Garden of Roses* as a cornet solo.' Space will not allow me to tell you of a dance, a 'carnival' procession, another race in which my daughter sailed against fourteen competitors and came in third. You'll be thinking that the sea hereabouts is real champagne and as the poet says, we

> Hear unconcernedly the oar
> That dips itself in wine.

On Friday I started our visitors on a Channel race to Falmouth; watched them away like a flight of white moths, sighed relief, packed up my gun—it was September 1st, but I hadn't hit a partridge—upped anchor and returned in the tug to the perusal (combined) of *David Copperfield* and Forster's *Life of Dickens*.

Q certainly enjoyed the annual regatta at Fowey, but what he enjoyed far more than anything else in the yearly round was Christmas, for which he prepared long in advance. On Christmas Eve the house had to be carefully decorated. On Christmas morning the family went to church. They spent the rest of the day at home and Q invariably passed part of the afternoon in his study, reading Hans Andersen's fairy tales. On Christmas Eve 1922 he wrote to H. F. Stewart, who was wintering in the South of France after a serious illness:

This is Christmas: a festival of great ceremonies in this small house: and I'll swear that even Les Agaves hasn't more beautiful sunshine than is pouring in here at this moment, and glancing up too from the sea at our feet, and playing heaven with the chrysanthemums and with the hollies, etc. on the pictures. And heaven will have to aid me in tackling the 'viands'. I have been shown successively, and with pride, a York ham, a huge foie gras, a box of kippers from Stornoway, and some 1848 Madeira which arrived a few weeks ago—the thoughtful donor having provided it with that interval for clarifying in the right temperature. My daughter—that mental sustenance should not be lacking either—has been searching England for the works of Ouida in the old three-volume first edition. (I hope you don't despise poor Ouida? She could be, and not seldom was, ridiculous: but was great all the same. Not a mean thought in her—would give herself away at any moment, like a prince tossing his best cloak to a beggar.) So I sit here barricaded with Ouida: and the family cat is basking outside on my window-ledge: and at 3 p.m. I have to lecture on Charles Dickens—which is a nuisance, but sounds Christmassy.

During the Christmas season Q and his family entertained extensively and were entertained by Fowey in return. In 1920, a few days after Christmas, they received an invitation to dine at the Fowey Hotel 'with a few friends'. On arrival at the hotel they were surprised to find that the friends were fifty-four in number and were all disguised as characters from Q's fiction—Simon Colliver, Claire Luttrell, Admiral Buzza, Miss Limpenny, Caleb Trotter, Jack Marvel, Joan of the Moor, Dorothea Westcote, Hetty Wesley, Nicky Vro, Marty Hymen, Lady Vyell, Captain Hocken, Captain Hunken, and many others. When all these had been presented to the family by the Mayor of Troy himself the company sat down to a menu every item of which (after a certain amount of manipulation of the French language) began with the letter Q. After dinner there were two toasts—'The Novels', proposed by Monsieur Charles Raoul, with a response by Miss Quiney, and 'The Author', proposed by the Reverend Samuel Wesley, who no doubt had some caustic remarks to make.

Although Q loved the festivities of Christmas greatly it was probably at this time of the year that he was most conscious of the gap that the war had left in the family circle. He felt his son's death so keenly that he could never trust himself to write about it. The wound that it had inflicted on his heart never healed completely. Despite himself, it would wring a cry from him at times, as when he said in All Saints' Church, Cambridge, on the fifth anniversary of Armistice Day:

There are few households in this land that this war has left without a domestic sorrow far more real, more natural, more abiding than any exultation over victory. All the old statues of Victory have wings: but Grief has no wings. She is the unwelcome lodger that squats on the hearth-stone between us and the fire and will not move or be dislodged.

Yet he was never selfish in his grief. When, nearly twenty years after the war had ended, some attempts were being made to suppress undergraduate frolics at Cambridge on Armistice Day, he wrote:

Elders and parents should, I hold, allow any amount of gladness to Armistice Day. For them, at any rate, All Souls' Day remains. Yet for most of them the pang, perhaps, will likelier start in some sudden moment when spring starts to reclothe the countryside but never for them to colour it with the promise spring brought in 1914.

The mare that Bevil Quiller-Couch had ridden throughout the war survived her master and Q succeeded in buying her from the War Office. He had her brought to Fowey, where he tended her carefully. When she died he hung a photograph of her on the wall of his keeping-room at Cambridge, just below a photograph of his son in military uniform. Occasionally a guest, whom Q's intimates had forgotten to warn not to do so, would ask questions about the two photographs. Q would answer him in a quiet voice and in the end would generally be overcome by emotion and retire to his bedroom.

Contristatus itaque rex ascendit coenaculum portae....

CHAPTER IX

THE SEXAGENARIAN (1923-33)

Q'S LITERARY output between his sixtieth and seventieth birthdays, though less extensive than during the previous ten years, was nevertheless considerable. It included two volumes of collected lectures and essays, a substantial anthology of English prose, a share in three Bible anthologies, and a new edition of his fiction in thirty volumes. It included also (as always) a number of generous Introductions to books by friends, acquaintances, old pupils, and others—and his Introductions to other men's books contain some of his most delicate and charming writing.

The Bible anthologies were published by the Cambridge University Press, of which S. C. Roberts had succeeded A. R. Waller as Secretary in 1922, with G. V. Carey as Educational Secretary. Two of the anthologies—*The Children's Bible* and *The Little Children's Bible*—were intended for use with a new syllabus of religious teaching that Q had helped to draw up for Cambridgeshire schools in 1923. The compilation of the anthologies was entrusted to three collaborators—Q, Alexander Nairne and T. R. Glover. Nairne was now Regius Professor of Divinity and Glover was Public Orator of the University and at the time President of the Baptist Union of Great Britain and Ireland. Towards Glover's rigid Nonconformity and teetotalism Q was not sympathetic. He nevertheless held the balance fairly between his two colleagues, who (he said) frequently disagreed strongly about the selection of Biblical passages, so that Glover sometimes addressed Nairne with clenched teeth. Q told Glover that he regarded himself as 'the pure white leaf in the Bible separating the Old and New Testaments'. Glover was pleased at the remark; but Q wrote afterwards: 'I wonder which Dispensation he supposed me to be assigning to him.'

The Children's Bible and *The Little Children's Bible* were published in 1924. Nairne and Glover were for pressing on at once with a third anthology, which was intended for adults. Q, however, refused (as always) to be hurried, and in January 1925 he wrote to S. C. Roberts from Fowey: 'I understand that in these halcyon days the Regius Professor of Divinity and the Public Orator are both sitting on the final egg of Father Carey's Chicken. The balance is insecure and the egg is like to be a Curate's Egg unless Carey and I (I say it modestly) do a bit of adjusting.' This 'final egg'—*The Cambridge Shorter Bible*—appeared in 1928. Its publication fulfilled Q's long-standing wish to arrange the text of the Bible in attractive literary form. It was nearly thirty years since he had written of the youthful heroine of his *Lady Good-for-Nothing* that 'the Bible was more alive to her because she had taken it like any other book, ignoring the Genevan division of verses and the sophisticated chapter headings. Thus studied, it had revenged itself by taking possession of her.'

The Children's Bible and *The Little Children's Bible* were hardly completed when Q began to have serious trouble with his eyesight, so that the final stages of his work on *The Oxford Book of English Prose* were carried out under great difficulties. In the autumn of 1924 he wrote: 'My eyes in these last two or three months have gone rapidly to grief and now glasses don't help me to read print.' His friends were greatly alarmed at the tragedy of blindness that seemed to be impending, but he himself faced the possibility of it with his usual calm. 'The thing *may* be curable', he wrote to S. C. Roberts. 'Anyway I've had a good time.' For a few terms he had to deliver his lectures extempore—a practice that he detested.

His new *Oxford Book* appeared in 1925 and was dedicated 'To two houses of learning and hospitality, Trinity College, Oxford, and Jesus College, Cambridge, and to friendship'. In his preface, he made it clear that he regarded *The Oxford Book of English Prose* as his swan song. He made his confidence in the younger generation equally clear—a confidence that was life-long. He said:

I propose that, with the aid of the Clarendon Press, this book shall be put on sale on November 25, 1925—twenty-five years to a day since the *Oxford Book of English Verse* saw the light and started to creep into public

recognition, at first (as I remember) very slowly. While no more superstitious than ordinary men, I take a pleasure in observing birthdays
and other private anniversaries as well as those of the Church: and
it is my fancy to choose this as an omen of continuance in some public
favour....

In covenant with the years, I have felt it right to concede that my
sympathy with prose nowadays being written, though often warm
enough, misses a right capacity to discriminate. Therefore I end this
book with writers who had already solidified their work by 1914, and
I trust that the reader will accept this break-off as reasonable and allow
me *donatum iam rude* to hang up just there the old harness. Yet, relin-
quishing it, I look forward in entire faith to the opening fields. The
Newspaper Press admits to-day a portentous amount of that Jargon or
flaccid writing to which flaccid thought instinctively resorts. But
literature, I repeat, is memorable speech, recording memorable thoughts
and deeds, and in such deeds at any rate the younger generation has not
failed....

So, taking leave of a trade which in these years has at least not lacked
the compliment of imitation, I look back somewhat wistfully on the
fields traversed, to be searched over by other eyes to which I would
fain bequeath, if I could so entreat the gods, a freshness of eyesight more
delicate than mine.

Q had been greatly helped in his preparation of *The Oxford Book
of English Prose* by Miss Winifred Hutchinson, a graduate of
Newnham College who lived at Cambridge and coached in Greek.
As she was widely read and had a remarkably good memory, she
was an ideal assistant for Q and had done secretarial work for him
ever since 1917, when he already had trouble with his eyes.
Miss Hutchinson shared a house in Bridge Street with her friend
Miss Rosamond Philpott, and the two ladies became firm friends
of Q. Every Whit Monday he used to hire a car and take them out
into the country for a picnic lunch—to the source of the Cam at
Ashwell, the Cambridgeshire downs at Heydon, or elsewhere.
One year he chose a riverside spot near Clare in Suffolk. The ladies
always remembered that picnic as the one of 'The Great Explosion
of Wrath'; for when Q opened the lunch basket to take out the
bottle of Burgundy that he had chosen with great care from the

THE HAVEN
FOWEY
　　CORNWALL. April 9th
'925

My dear Stewart

Yes. Bridges has a
noble view (and a noble wife,
forbye). Whether or no the old
ruffian deserves his luck I don't
say. He's a spoilt child; but I
like him, & he permits my unholy mirth
when he gets too oracular. Still — &
to confine oneself to the view — if the
6th Commandment were extended against
coveting one's neighbour's Fiesole, I
should get off with a caution : for I
want a straight horizon line of sea, some
-where & not very far and water at one's
feet and noiseless vessels coming & going
or swinging at anchor. So that my
view is always the same & yet has

differed hourly in its components, never one
repeated itself since the first syllable of
recorded time. But that Vale with the
spires & dome is exquisite: perhaps best
of all on an April day with sun & shadow
chasing each other over it. I have been
spending the time (a) cutting brambles, knee
deep in such daffodils — or ankle deep in
such primroses; (b) visiting schools & sitting
on C. Council Committees; (c) writing at
novel as well as my poor eyes will allow:
and (d) Exploring — or rather renewing old
explorations of the real scene of the
Tristan & Iseult business. Yes, my boy
— the real scene. Is there anything in the
world jollier than happening on a little ting[?]
of confirmatory evidence that has lain latent

for hundreds of years & dodged the antiquarians
last week when I was morally certain where
King Mark's Castle must have stood, the
farmer's wife at the manor farm below, over
a hospitable tea pot out some deeds & a
map with the names of the fields on it;
and lo! the meadow exactly fitting my
hypothesis was named 'Mark's Gate!'
An adjoining small field — on which the postern
should have opened has for name, 'Pilfer
Parc " Plus ça change —
I think this discovery deserves a votive
offering : and since I understand that
the Clergy are not above Easter Offerings,
I am asking you to accept, on its
account . a vol. of Leclisse _ on Dickens
& other Victorians   which shall
follow by separate parcel . You'll like
my liking for D. even when you dissent
from some observations.
        Jenkinson's will be a tricky Memoir

to write. But don't leave that remark on Ld Acton out. He was just like that. So was the late Charles Dilke — knew everything & would tell you anything you didn't want to know, with a finality that killed conversation. Sort of archiepiscopal vulpicides posted on the edge of a covert and promptly shooting dead every fox you put up, while you — poor hound — ran back & howled in Gladstro, with a few shot of their bounty scattered into your own posterior.

I am afraid Miss Hutchinson has been rather seriously ill. Please tell Madonna with my "humble duty" that I was very sorry indeed not to keep that engagement for luncheon last term. But the doctor put me to bed & threatened a night nurse. I preferred strong brandy hot, & won.

Yours ever
Q.

College cellar he found that some abominable teetotal drink had been packed in its place by mistake.

In spite of his eye-trouble Q was at this time planning a new novel, called *Castle d'Or*, the scene of which he laid near St Winnow on the River Fowey in the late eighteenth century. He refers to it in a letter that he wrote during the Easter vacation of 1925 to H. F. Stewart, who had been calling on Robert Bridges at his Oxford house on Boar's Hill:

Yes, Bridges has a noble view (and a noble wife, forbye). Whether or no the old ruffian deserves his luck I don't say. He's a spoilt child; but I like him, and he permits my unholy mirth when he gets too oracular. Still—and to confine myself to the view—if the Tenth Commandment were extended to coveting one's neighbour's Fiesole, I should get off with a caution: for *I* want a straight horizon line of sea somewhere and not very far and water at one's feet and noiseless vessels coming and going or swinging at anchor; so that *my* view is always the same and yet has differed hourly in its components, never once repeated itself since the first syllable of recorded time. But that vale with the spires and dome is exquisite: perhaps best of all on an April day with sun and shadow chasing each other over it.

I have been spending the time (*a*) cutting brambles, knee-deep in *such* daffodils or ankle-deep in *such* primroses; (*b*) visiting schools and sitting on County Council committees; (*c*) writing at a novel as well as my poor eyes will allow; and (*d*) exploring—or rather renewing old explorations of the real scene of the Tristan and Iseult business. Yes, my boy—the real scene. Is there anything in the world jollier than happening on a little trifle of confirmatory evidence that has lain latent for hundreds of years and dodged the antiquarians? Last week when I was morally certain where King Mark's castle must have stood, the farmer's wife at the manor farm below, over a hospitable cup of tea got out some deeds and a map with the names of fields on it; and lo! the meadow exactly fitting my hypothesis was named 'Mark's Gate'. An adjoining small field, on which the postern should have opened, has for name 'Pilfer Parc'. *Plus ça change*....

In the summer of the same year J. M. Barrie, who had heard alarming reports of the state of Q's eyesight, spent a day with him at Cambridge and walked down to the May Races with him. He wrote to Q afterwards: 'The one regrettable thing about my visit is that we did not have a long evening alone together when we could have come closer to each other, as I am sure we both wanted. And how tongue-tied was I when we were going to the station and at it! Yet I was full of affection for you then, and I can't tell you how sorry I am that you have this trouble with your eyes. I could have made so much more of my time, but nevertheless it was to me the happiest visit I have paid anywhere for a very long time.'

In December Q wrote to S. C. Roberts: 'I believe my term as a Syndic [of the University Press] expires this year. It will ease matters if you just understand that I wish to go out as, by gentle process, out of everything.' During the early months of 1926 his eyesight seemed to get even worse; and then, by the middle of the summer, it quite unexpectedly showed great improvement. Q himself dated the improvement from the time when an oculist whom he had consulted delighted him by countermanding the prohibition of tobacco which until then had formed part of his treatment. By the end of 1927 his eyesight seemed as good as it had ever been and it never again gave cause for anxiety. By the irony of fate, Miss Hutchinson, who had been so great a helper to him in his trouble, was herself stricken with blindness after-wards. Q used to visit her frequently until she left Cambridge with Miss Philpott a few years later; and he continued to write cheering, chivalrous letters to her until she died at Wells in 1937.

In the same year as *The Oxford Book of English Prose* Q published his *Charles Dickens and Other Victorians*, which consisted almost entirely of lectures delivered at Cambridge. He then began to prepare a new uniform edition of his fiction. This appeared in 1928–9 as 'The Duchy Edition', in thirty volumes, with a new preface to practically every volume.

It was a bold step to republish thirty volumes of fiction by a single writer—some of them over forty years old. What made it even bolder was that literary fashions and tastes had changed greatly since the war of 1914–18. There was a demand for novels with unpleasant settings, novels with a strong sex interest, novels that played with psycho-analysis, novels and biographies that 'debunked' human life and character. Q was well aware that his fiction lacked all these features: in the new prefaces to the 'Duchy Edition' he made it quite plain that he was glad of it and that he was convinced that public taste would turn back in time to better themes.

In his preface to *I Saw Three Ships*, for instance, he said:

I understand that since the War there has grown up a revulsion against the sort of plain adventurous story. I have chosen always, and made it my freedom, to write on themes that interested me. Monkey-houses do not, and psycho-analysis does not. If an arrogant fashion in criticism choose to pass my work over as therefore negligible—well, it must for the time. My stories simply treat men and women, with their differences, as I have been allowed their acquaintance in life.

In the preface to *Poison Island*, with its straightforward humour and adventure, he attacked contemporary fiction that mimicked Russian plays like *Uncle Vanya*. 'The now fashionable Russian trick of endless talk which never arrives at action cannot endure', he wrote. 'It satisfies us rather, though the conclusion be abrupt, to see the curtain fall on a stage piled with corpses than on a typical Russian hero who, after three hours of self-exploration, crawls out of the window as his last way of escape from doing anything whatever.'

In the preface to *Two Sides of the Face* he defended humorous writing, which seemed to be at a discount at the time. 'The present fashion among critics', he said, 'is to treat no artists seriously but those who pull long faces; and it will not matter to me very much how long the fashion endures. . . . I hold (after my experience) that the capacity to tell poignantly the tragedy of life and the acquired play of humour upon it are equally of divine communication and equally respectable.'

Perhaps his best apologia of all was the one contained in his preface to *The White Wolf*:

I have still—and at my time of life it may pardonably be asserted— the assurance that I have been able, in various ways, to touch many hearts, and am still able to touch some. They are few, perhaps, just now; and may yet dwindle, while professors tell us of 'the Romantic Movement' as though a spirit enjoyed a period, to pass into a dead thing, to be classified....

Any clever fellow can pull faces at humanity and deride it; as anyone with little expense can invent mishaps and misunderstandings. A novelist who traffics with sex and suicide, domestic bickerings and disillusions, is playing the very easiest game in the world. Any illiterate can make a hit with such a theme, if his mind be of the sort to descend to it. But to people a wide stage with characters at once good (as most are) and brave, in patience or adventure—*that* is the artist's test, as it seems to me. It means that in growing he has learnt to judge his fellow-sinners charitably, and to help them, before he leaves a world of all sorts in which it has been worth while to live.

Although he spoke gravely, sometimes even angrily, about the psycho-analytical school they nevertheless provided him with much amusement. It was at their expense that he wrote the limerick:

> Two students of psycho-analysis
> Corresponded on sexual fallacies
> Till confusion arose,
> And now nobody knows
> Which Algernon was or which Alice is.

His limericks and similar short rhymes were mostly composed on railway-station platforms in Cornwall, while he was waiting for trains to carry him about the county on his Education Committee work. Sometimes the name of the station would suggest a rhyme, as when he was waiting for a train at Roche:

> There was an old madman of Roche
> Who woke from a dream in a coach.
> He said to his neighbour:
> 'Division of labour!
> I've just laid an egg. Can you poach?'

As a sexagenarian, he was busier than he had ever been with Cornish educational affairs, for in 1923 he succeeded R. G. Rows as Chairman of the County Education Committee and he continued in office for eight years. In 1927 the Committee held a special Education Week to celebrate the twenty-fifth anniversary of the passing of the Balfour Education Act of 1902. A handbook to the celebration was drawn up and Q wrote a preface for it. This preface epitomizes so well Q's views on education and the work that he himself had done for Cornish schools, and provides so good a review of the great change that had come over elementary and secondary education in Cornwall and elsewhere in the course of twenty-five years, that it is quoted here in full:

Certain Cornishmen and Cornishwomen, believers in Education, who now for twenty-five years—some from the start, others in succession—have worked hard to build a system in our Duchy well and truly laid upon the basis of the Balfour Act of 1902 and using material provided by subsequent Acts of Parliament when these offered more than promises, have agreed that the time has arrived for challenging their countrymen to come and with open eyes judge some results of their labours. *That* is the meaning of our Education Week.

Of course the best results of Education can never be visible: its best results can never, in the nature of things, be visible. One may point to a fine building of stone set in a starved parish; to sanitation where before there was none; to airy well-windowed rooms (quite usually gay with flowers brought by the scholars) superseding loft or cellar where the upper standards sat at work cramped over half-lit deforming desks, or the infant class chanted in melancholy unison upon a 'gallery' infested with dust and germs. This we can point to, of course, and we can show it, so far as our Local Education Authority has had the care of the children's physical well-being freely consigned to it, over the length and across the breadth of Cornwall. Obviously we cannot centre such evidence in Truro or any one spot, as neither could we centre the acres of playing-fields acquired, or exhibit in a nexus our Secondary School system (inaugurated by our first Chairman, Mr R. G. Rows), the very first principle of which was missionary—that it should radiate out over a County measuring from Bude to Lizard, near a hundred miles, so if we could provide it, the missionary centres of Higher Education should be, through our sparse and scattered folk and over a land of moors and intersecting sea-creeks, planted within reasonable access of every Cornish child who could win his way through a Minor Scholarship to opportunities we would make his birthright. Well, again in the nature of things, we cannot bring these results together, to astonish the eye with congregated stone and mortar. But if by some Aladdin's lamp we could, we should still be cheating the spectator, falsifying the true soul of our aim. Nay, even if we have an imagination to deal with figures, and we prove to him by figures that his County Council owns, in land and buildings, well over a million of money, that its buildings alone could not be replaced, the children re-housed under less than two millions tomorrow, and that this property is administered by its Education Committee under vigilant eyes—not to mention the endless adjustments of staff and their payments, appointments, enquiries into grievances, constant visits and talks with Governors, Managers, Teachers, to make sure that the machinery is working sweetly—even so the last secret would be hid.

For the last secret lies hidden in the children: and we who work for Education are condemned always to be working on faith—on the evidence of things not seen. The whole inherently forbids nor can the true secret be exhibited or divulged.

For it resides somewhere in the heart—or mind—or both, of a boy or girl, and may even lie latent for years to be resurrected and to reform a life. It may lie enclosed in a sentence, almost in a word—casually dropped by some kindly teacher—to quicken at once or lie long in a half-remembrance before awakening, to germinate. It may be of wheat or of some other grain, and that which the teacher sows may not be quickened except to die....I have myself had the great happiness to abide a good part of my life within two great Universities, to walk under their walls and eat at tables upon which the portraits of great men looked down; and have daily felt that privilege as a wonder. But still more wonderful, more penetrating, and as experience has taught me more *enlightening* (if I may claim to have sought enlightenment on the path through life) have been certain remembered words of certain teachers who, as in remembered whispers of the *genius loci* which they had inherited, have stayed with those and stayed with me by green pastures out of old college rooms, quiet gardens.

This secret—the secret that may sound through life on the echo of a cracked school bell and draw a man back to re-visit a dingy class-room as, once, a spiritual birth place—can never be exhibited, can never challenge public admiration, can never expose immediate results in the market place; and this for the simple reason that it is a spirit which, like the wind, blows where it lists. I am sure—I have proved over many years—that it blows through many of our remotest schools.

But one thing even concerning this spirit we can put forward as a plain challenge. No observant man of my age, not being a crank, can deny that the children are better housed, fed, taught than they were forty years ago, or that their lives are happier. Those who originally fought against our setting up of Secondary Schools, and so fiercely that, as I have since reminded them, we had to build with the sword in one hand and the trowel in the other, are now pressing us to build more. We shall probably not build another for many years to come, but occupy ourselves, rather, with a steady improvement of the existing ones towards an ideal of perfection, and with opening roads of access to the Universities, especially to our own University of the South West of England, and with tuning up our Elementary Schools to a pitch of work *and* play not realized yet. And the Managers have come to think with us. If our old opponents will now look into their own hearts I think they will confess that any return to old conditions were unthinkable.

And we of the Local Education Authority, if we in our turn would look into our own hearts for a rebuke to self-complacency, should admit that in the beginning we wasted many months over bitter and barren sectarian debates, until the mute appeal of the children somehow became audible, and the reproach shook us together into a body with one strong purpose—I can even recall the day and hour when this miracle happened. It was the children who wrought it, the children who taught us; and it must be the children who, in Education Week, will reward us with our visible justification, all unconsciously pleading for us to the public with their healthy frames, refined movements, graceful rivalries, happy faces.

Q resigned the Chairmanship of the Education Committee in 1931, though he stayed on another three years as Vice-Chairman. Early in 1931 he wrote to a friend:

It was high time, really, that I resigned my Chairmanship of the Education Committee. I had been wanting to do it for some time, and only held on because the clerical managers had come to trust me to 'see fair'—never once having voted to close a Church School while it could be kept open without harm to the children's health. Also, the mere fact of one's being a Churchman (however suspect) and *not* a Wesleyan was always something of a help. That's why I didn't clear out altogether: there being, I think, an understanding that I can still be used in smoothing out the Hadow report.

In the following December he wrote:

I am gradually loosing all ties of the Education Committee. To begin with, my job at Cambridge has grown and takes up my thoughts; and secondly I have a feeling that all I've tried to do on the Committee has really been in vain—all except the prolonged fight for fair treatment of the Church Elementary Schools: which is just what will never be recognized by the clergy. For the rest, I must give up fighting with local preachers at Ephesus....Moreover I have been considering the Income Tax and find that I must *work*. Well, that's no hardship: and I like it ever so much better than Committee meetings.

When Q severed his connection with the Education Committee in 1934 he did not cease to take an interest in Cornish education, but he limited his active educational work to Fowey, where he was a Governor of the Grammar School and for twelve years President of the local branch of the Workers' Educational Association. He addressed the latter at least once during practically every session throughout his presidency and made the members feel (as one of them expressed it) 'in the position of intimate students gathered in his own college rooms'.

His activities, educational and other, were by no means limited to Cornwall and Cambridge. Naturally, he went fairly often to Oxford—to deliver lectures to University Extension students, for instance, to attend conferences of the Village Drama Society or other bodies, or for sheer pleasure. His visits to Oxford became more frequent after 1926, when (to his great satisfaction) his old college elected him to an Honorary Fellowship. Honours from farther afield came to him in 1927, when the University of Aberdeen conferred an honorary degree on him, and in 1930, when the University of Edinburgh, of which Barrie had just been elected Chancellor, did the same.

His sense of duty, his kindness of heart, and his personal tastes led him to accept engagements to deliver lectures or speeches in many parts of the country. During the period between the end of the war and 1933 we find him going to London to address the Dickens Fellowship, the Newspaper Society and the London Cornish Association, to lecture on Shakespeare to the British Academy, to give an address at the opening of Keats House, Hampstead, and to distribute the prizes at Leyton County High School, of which his cousin, Dr L. Couch, was the headmaster; to Plymouth to address a conference of the National Union of Journalists, to talk to the Rotary Club about the ancient universities, and to preside over an annual meeting of a local hospital; to Exeter, Tonbridge and Guildford to address meetings of the Village Drama Society; to Tewkesbury to speak about Mrs Craik; to Aberystwyth to lecture on 'The Value of Poetry'; to Bishop Stortford School to open a new hall and chapel; to Caistor in Lincolnshire to speak at the tercentenary of the Grammar School, at which his friend and colleague, Bernard Manning, had been educated; to South Mymms to get local colour before writing an Introduction to a history of the parish; to Bedford to open a new library in the Girls' High School; to Nottingham to inaugurate a Byron Lectureship at University College; to Eton College to inspect the English work; to Sevenoaks School to distribute prizes and give an address on Virgil; and to Edinburgh to preside over an annual meeting of the Sir Walter Scott Club.

This list of engagements, which is not exhaustive, could no doubt be paralleled in the lives of other literary men. What is striking about Q's formal public speeches, however, is not so much their number as the very high standard that they maintained. Printed records and the testimony of persons who were present show that he never lapsed. The size of the gathering made no difference: his speeches were works of art. They were always prepared with the greatest care, they were beautifully phrased, and they fitted the occasion perfectly.

Consider, for instance, the moving exordium of his address at the opening of Keats House:

First let me congratulate you, Mr Mayor, upon the occasion.

> There may be cities that refuse
> To their own child his honours due,

but Hampstead is not one of these. Always in Hampstead, going by its walks or on the edge of its heath, any man of letters must be haunted by thoughts which seem to him almost memories: of a great literary tradition merging still—please Heaven!—into a great literary future. Still of the town, yet not of the town—but fragrant, on the country's rim—these ghosts, thoughts, memories, accompany or tread close on the musing mind. A statue or an obelisk were an offence to the *genius loci*; which pursues rather along the shade of a paling or under a tree that in a time before ours once

in a drear-nighted December

showed a part of its frosted branches to the lamp-light, or in spring budded to arrest a poet's step on your pathways or broke into leaf and held, on this verge of London, an immortal nightingale captive.

And so, Sir, it is surely to Hampstead's credit that you have chosen, instead of obelisk or statue, to preserve this simple house in perpetuity for a memorial of John Keats. In this house he agonized with love and despondency: on a bed in a chamber above us he read in a drop of blood his death warrant: from the door beyond that passage he departed on his last journey—brave and hopeless as Henry Fielding on *his* last voyage. In the dim garden outside yonder pane of glass he heard the Hampstead nightingale and translated that song 'not born for death' into human speech as near heavenly as any we can dare to snatch out of this transitory life to call immortal. Still on the edge and shadow of that trench untimely digged we invoke that genius, fleet as water, 'writ in water'.

Still are thy pleasant voices, thy nightingales, awake:
For Death he taketh all away: but them he cannot take.

'Men are we and must mourn.' *Mentem mortalia tangunt.* But here, Sir, in this room—in this house—you preserve almost all that a decent, necessary piety can preserve.

The man who could appeal thus to 'a little clan' of devotees of a poets' poet could go equally straight to the heart of the band of schoolboys who were gathered perforce to listen to him at Sevenoaks School:

I foresee trouble, or at least a danger of awaking suspicions (which, however, your good manners will conceal), in the opening words of my little address. You have all been reading in the papers that Virgil was born two thousand years ago on October 15th, and it is possible that some of my hearers—say in the Lower School or on the Modern Side— may not respond whole-heartedly to the rejoicings of the civilized world over that happy event. Indeed I have been a fourth-form boy and have known companions who audibly regretted that the event had ever occurred: and at any rate I scarcely expect *all* Rome to send forth a rapturous cry at the mention of Virgil's name, while even the ranks of Tuscany (whatever part of your school they represent) may find little or no difficulty in forbearing to cheer.

Be reassured. It is now some forty years since I gave up lecturing on Virgil: and if I invoke the sacred name this afternoon it shall be but to remind you of certain resemblances between his youth and yours, his land and this Kent of yours, with certain traditions which some of us like to consider as part of our inheritance from Rome: which are as valid to-day as two thousand years ago, and (for our present purpose) should be sacramental to any boy with a heart set on the increase of this ancient school in repute, or at least on leaving it (as the old Athenian said of his estate) 'not worse, but something better than he found it'.

Unlike many literary men, Q was not addicted to writing letters to newspapers; but on the comparatively few occasions when he did so the result was admirable, as in the beautiful letter which he wrote to *The Times* on the death of Kenneth Grahame:

> The Haven,
> Fowey.
> 14 *July*, 1932

Sir,

In the obituaries of Kenneth Grahame one misses (though friendship may be exacting) full recognition of his personal charm and the beauty —there is no other word—of his character. This, of course, could be divined in his books, few, yet in their way surely classical; but he avoided publicity always, in later years kept deeper retirement under a great sorrow; and so, perhaps, as these books must by their nature have attracted many readers towards a further intimacy of which he was shy, a word or two about him may be acceptable to them and pardonable by his spirit. One does not, anyhow, wish to go out of this world without acknowledging one of the best things found in it.

He came to these parts and to this house (from which he was afterwards married) a little more than thirty years ago; convalescent from a severe illness. Lazy afternoons at sea completed his recovery and made me acquainted with a man who combined all enviable gifts and yet so perfectly as to soften all envy away in affection. Noble in looks, yet modest in bearing; with flashes of wit that played at call around any subject, lambent as summer lightning, never hurting, and with silences that half-revealed things beyond reach of words, he seemed at once a child and a king. Withal he was eminently a 'man's man' and keen on all manly sports: a man, too, who—as Secretary of the Bank of England —knew much of practical affairs and could judge them incisively if with amusement, while his own mind kept its loyalty to sweet thoughts, great manners, and a quiet disdain of anything meaner than these. I must remember him as a 'classical' man, perfectly aware of himself as 'at best a noble plaything of the gods', whose will he seemed to understand through his gift of interpreting childhood.

His *Wind in the Willows* had its origin in a series of weekly letters invented to amuse the school-time of his only son, whose loss in undergraduate prime at Oxford broke the parents' life. But though his roof had fallen, the pillar stood upright.

I have a feeling, Sir, that many who loved his books without the privilege of having known him privately will be glad to hear (as I am permitted to tell) that Kenneth Grahame's end was sudden, peaceful, and painless. On Tuesday, the 5th, after an evening walk with his wife, he had retired and was reading in bed when the stroke fell with a sudden haemorrhage of the brain. The book slipped from his hand to the floor and he slept out of life to the murmur of the Thames by Pangbourne.

I am, Sir, your obedient servant,

ARTHUR QUILLER-COUCH.

Q's letters to his friends, though generally less polished than those intended for publication, make excellent reading. They frequently give entertaining accounts of Cornish life and sketches of Cornish characters, both lay and clerical. Q often asserted that many of the Cornish clergy were 'mad as sheep'. In this category he very understandably included Bernard Walke, whom he had known when he was curate of Lanteglos-by-Fowey, in which parish Polruan is included. Walke was afterwards Vicar of the parish of

St Hilary, where his eccentricities caused violent disputes and law-suits. Q refers to them in the following letter to H. F. Stewart:

The Haven,
Fowey.
August 29th 1932.

...A heavenly summer down here. Many more 'visitors' than ever, but the balance almost redeemed by the slightness of their clothing; and so, as the saying is, we make it up on the wear-abouts. But the bad spate seems to have been diverted, for advertisement purposes, on to poor St Hilary.

I wonder if some good will come of this wretched business? On the one hand you have the Kensit folk, bank-holiday cads to the bone and revolting all of us by their obscenity: on the other my old friend Bernard Walke, who never in my long acquaintance could envisage any sort of law (even to a modest request on a notice-board) as not inviting defiance: and cornered, because he cannot quite say out what he really believes—that the one ultimate authority over the Church of England is the Bishop of Rome (and he'd be just as likely to obey *him* as G. B. Shaw would be to abide by any law laid down at his advice by a Socialist State of his own invention). I hope you won't mind my saying that 'tis a pity the saints are so often *sly*.

At this moment we are full of business here, on the eve of regattas: with three of the great racers here—*Candida, Astra* and *Westward,* and heaps of others—the harbour all be-jewelled of nights, and the lanterns of the pilchard fleet all drawn like a—by the way, what *is* a carcenet? Anyway, I stick to it that the lights in the offing are the jeweller's goods.

I believe I am to be your (The Society's) host on October 17th. It crossed my mind the other night, as I lay tossing in bed with this thought, that a boiled leg of Spanish hog (Don Quixote's country, chaud-froid) with a cheese salad of which I share the secret with three men only— (An interval. Knocking without. Several persons from Porlock enter thirstily on their way to or from the Land's End. *Air,* 'Old English hospitality was never known to fail', but I wish I could be certain the host won't, at this rate.)...

The Sexagenarian (1923–33)

A year later, when Q had once more been interrupted by callers from Porlock, he wrote:

Fowey,

September 13th 1933.

I hope Stanley Baldwin will come up for *Ad Eundem* in November and stay with me...

Idly turning the pages of my blotter while pondering a sentence for a *Times Lit. Supp.* article on Tennyson in 1833—you will see it in to-morrow's issue for additional proof that I am alive though torpid— I came on the first half of a longish letter composed in response to your kind advances of 13th ult. It hasn't quite the literary merit of *Xanadu*: on the other hand it was not written under the influence of opium: the main point of similarity being that both were interrupted by a person or persons 'from Porlock'.

Oh, these visitors !—But now at least they are clearing out and taking their brats back to school: and now above an empty harbour we are wrestling with a plum and apple crop the like of which I have never known. Five afternoons have we worked in the hot sun and have gathered a quarter of the crop, if so much. What a summer, too ! but not torrid here. The grass is quite green and the fuchsias in great bloom. To-morrow I get a respite from manual labour—opening of a Girl's School in the afternoon, and in the evening a journey into the far country, to talk to a Women's Institute about the history of their parish....

I wonder more and more how any man, as he nears seventy, can find —either at Cambridge or in the depths of the country—a spare hour for improving his own mind or, for that matter, for doing any concentrated work. I brought home Aristotle his *Rhetoric* and a lot of Cambridge Platonist stuff—instead of which I've been opening swimming baths, Church bazaars, regattas—and at my back I alwaies hear Time's winged chariot—an apple-cart these five days—hurrying near, and get to bed tired out with the beginnings of a beautiful lyric in my head—quite gone on awaking.

...I propose to enjoy your hospitality on October 16th if in the meantime you haven't removed to Eton, whither I shall unhappily be unable to follow you; since they did away, a while ago, with the Naval Knights of Windsor: reason (according to Nairne) that when drunk they used to unstrap and beat one another with their wooden legs. If that's so, even in the old days I lacked one of the two qualifications.

At Cambridge, even when his eyesight was at its worst, Q continued with his weekly Aristotle classes and with many of his social engagements. In 1925, for instance, he was one of those who gave a lunch in honour of Gustave David, the Cambridge book-seller. David had sold books in the market place for many years on four days a week. On Thursdays he went to London to attend book sales; and on Saturdays, as Q put it, 'when the merry costers invaded the market, like some grave Tyrian trader he withdrew to the neighbouring eminence of Pease Hill, and there, among the fried fish stalls, undid his corded bales'.

A few years later, Q received an invitation to a lunch of a very different kind. The invitation came from an ecclesiastical body and the company was to be a large one. From what he knew of those who were going to be present, Q strongly suspected that, although the lunch was to be at a hotel, it would be a strictly teetotal affair. Before accepting the invitation he asked his retainer, Henry Stubbings—a quaint little bearded man of eighty, who used to run errands for him—if he could discover whether his suspicion was well founded.

'Certainly, Sir Arthur', Henry answered. 'I can easily find out about that. You see, the head waiter there is a relation of mine.'

An hour or so later Henry came back and said: 'Yes, Sir Arthur, the lunch is going to be teetotal, but the head waiter says it will be all right.'

'Did he explain what he meant by being "all right," Henry?' Q asked.

'Well, Sir Arthur, as far as I could understand he meant it would be all right for you,' Henry answered.

So Q accepted the invitation and found himself sitting at a table with several teetotallers. When the lunch began the waiters went round and asked the guests whether they would take ginger beer, lemonade, or water; but they passed Q by without saying anything. Q also held his peace and soon afterwards a hand appeared over his shoulder and poured something into his glass. When he tasted it, he found it was lemonade well laced with gin.

After a while his neighbour at table said: 'Your lemonade looks a different colour from mine, Sir Arthur.'

'Yes', said Q, 'it's a special lemonade. Would you like to try it? Good! Waiter, bring this gentleman some of that special lemonade, please.'

'My word!' said the other man when he had tasted it. 'This is wonderful lemonade. I've never tasted any as good as this before. I wonder if I could get the recipe. Marvellous lemonade Sir Arthur's got here,' he said to another luncher at the same table.

'Could I taste it, please?' the third man asked.

'Certainly', said Q. 'Waiter, bring this gentleman some of that special lemonade, please.'

Before long, everyone at the table was drinking Q's special lemonade. There is nothing more to the story. No one became inebriated, but before the lunch was over there was general recognition that the wittiest remarks and the warmest good feeling in the room came from Q's table.

Q's comfort at Jesus College was greatly increased in 1931, when the lecture-room that was separated from his rooms only by a staircase was converted into a set of rooms for the accommodation of Fellows' guests. The furnishing and decorating of the rooms were supervised by Q, who chose a carpet and wallpaper of an uncommon shade of red. It was agreed between him and the College that he (in return for a rent) could have the full use of this new set of rooms when it was not being used for a guest. Q therefore always insisting on describing the guest room as 'my dining room'. The facetious often called it 'the Q-bicle'. Here Q kept the overflow of his books and held his numerous lunch parties, dinner parties and meetings of some of the clubs to which he belonged, such as the Red Herrings.

The Red Herrings formed the 'upper perch' of a Jesus College social club called the Roosters, to which Q had been elected in 1930. The club derived its name from John Alcock, Bishop of Ely, the founder of the College, and its members were predominantly undergraduates, with a sprinkling of dons. Q, who held the office of High Steward of the Roost, did not attend the normal meetings of the club regularly, but he appeared at the dinners and similar functions, wearing his Red Herring tie and black skull cap adorned with a red herring without being in the least self-conscious. He always attended what the Roosters called their Annual Fair and opened it with a mock-serious speech; and every year he helped to write humorous lyrics for the Roosters' Revue —a stage burlesque of the history of the College. He never missed a 'Shoal' of the Red Herrings, who met in 'the Q-bicle' after dinner for dessert, wine, and talk, with punch following in the winter. Great care had to be taken to see that there were never thirteen persons present, because Q was superstitious about that number. On one occasion, when someone brought the party up to thirteen by unexpectedly introducing a guest, there was a whispered consultation outside the room before Q realized how many were present and it was arranged that the junior members should be absent by turns for half an hour during the rest of the evening so as to avoid the forbidden number.

One of the earliest functions to take place in 'my dining room' was a lunch given by Q and some other senior members of the College in honour of Mr F. J. Sebley, on his retirement after forty years' service with Messrs Heffer, the Cambridge booksellers. Nairne, who was one of the hosts, characteristically paid his share of the cost but stayed away from the lunch because he could not face the food. After the lunch the Master, Arthur Gray, rose to propose the health of the guest of honour. He knew both Mr Heffer and Mr Sebley very well, but was apt to be absent-minded. Accordingly, throwing (as he always did) great emphasis on every third or fourth word, he said:

'It gives us *great* pleasure, gentlemen, to have with us to-*day* our *good* friend, Mr *Heffer*.' (Here Q plucked him by the sleeve and spoke to him in stage whispers.) 'What's that, Q? *Not* Mr Heffer? Very *well*, then. As I was saying, it gives us *great* pleasure to be here to-*day* to do honour to our *good* friend, Mr *Heffer*.' (More sleeve-plucking.) '*What* did you say, Q? *Not* Mr Heffer? *Quite* so. How stupid of me! Definitely *not* Mr Heffer. Very *well*,

then. It gives all of us *great* pleasure to have with us to-*day*
our *good* friend Mr — our *good* friend who has done so
much for us for *many* years. We are *very* glad to have with us
to-*day* our friend Mr Heffer.' (Here Q gave up the sleeve-
plucking as hopeless.) 'I ask you to *rise* with me and drink to
his *health*. Gentlemen, Mr *Heffer*!' And the company rose and
drank to the health of Mr Sebley, who was as much amused as
anyone.

Sebley and David, being devoted to the memory of S. T.
Coleridge, were both invited to a Coleridge celebration that
was held at Jesus (the poet's old college) in 1933. The College
originally intended to hold the celebration in 1934, the centenary
of the poet's death, but Foakes-Jackson, who wished to be present,
found that it would be more convenient for him to cross the
Atlantic from New York in 1933. The College therefore brought
the commemoration forward a year, and Arthur Gray described it
in a happy phrase as a quasi-centenary. Foakes-Jackson gave a
bronze of Coleridge to be placed in the College chapel. It was cast by
Gilbert Coleridge—Q's old friend at Oxford, and Foakes-Jackson's
fag at Eton—who was descended from the poet's brother. Q made
a beautiful speech at the unveiling of the bronze, but unfortunately
the manuscript was not preserved. Sebley listened intently to the
after-dinner speeches in the College hall that evening, while David
sat fast asleep with a cigar in his mouth.

Q was in his element on such occasions as the Coleridge dinner
and was in constant demand at college feasts throughout the
University. At Jesus College there were normally two feasts a
year—the Audit and the Rustat. Unfortunately, he was never
present at the Audit Feast, as it took place a very few days before
Christmas—long after he had departed for Fowey. He never, on
the other hand, missed the Rustat Feast, which took place in the
middle of the May Term, and he generally brought a couple of
guests, of whom either H. F. Stewart or S. C. Roberts was fairly
sure to be one. Sometimes A. E. Housman was his guest. On one
occasion when he invited Housman he received the following
reply:

The Sexagenarian (1923–33)

Trinity College.
9 May 1929.

My dear Q,

I am annoyed to find that Tuesday the 14th is a date when I am engaged to dine at Christ's. I wish that colleges would show more concern for gluttons and drunkards in arranging their Feasts.

Yours,

A. E. HOUSMAN.

For one reason or another Q always stayed at Cambridge later in the May term than in the other terms. If Jesus College finished Head of the River he attended the bump supper. He did not attend the May Week ball but he nearly always stayed until the ball was over and the dancers had been photographed in a big group under his windows by early morning light while he was still sound asleep. The photograph had for its background the thousands of flowers on the René Andrée rose that he had brought from Fowey in 1913 and planted under his windows. It had flourished there and had grown until it covered a great expanse of wall and extended its branches round the end of the building to the far side.

Everything that Q did was done thoroughly, with no unnecessary haste, and with a gravity under the surface of which a sense of humour always lurked. Even the buying of a tie was a small ceremony with him; and his going down at the end of term was an event which no one who took part in it could ever forget. It was generally attended by the President and other chief officers of the Roosters. When the porters had entered Q's room and removed a remarkable number of trunks, boxes of books, suitcases, and valises for the journey, a glass of sherry would be distributed all round and there was much talking and laughter. At a signal given from the Porter's Lodge on the far side of the court, Q's gyp would enter the room and announce that the car had arrived. Q would then put on his grey, brown, or black bowler hat, adjusting it carefully in the glass—he was perhaps the last man in England to wear bowlers of different colours to match his suits—and would hand to one of the company the spare bowler with which he generally travelled to and from Cornwall. He would then go out of the room, taking off his hat again as soon as he got outside the door in order to say goodbye to his bedmaker. The whole company, varying in number from half a dozen to a dozen or more, then went across First Court and down the Chimney to the car at the outer gate. Here Q would say goodbye to the majority of the company, but a few of the higher officers were allowed to go with him to the railway station. Everyone there, from the stationmaster downwards, seemed to be very willingly at his beck and call, and the train did not move until he had found a compartment that suited him and the luggage and spare bowler had been safely stowed. An inspection of the train was sometimes necessary before a suitable compartment could be found: it was impressive to see Q, accompanied by the station-master, the guard, a couple of porters and the party from Jesus College, perambulating the platform as he carried out his grave and unhurried inspection.

In the summer, Lady Quiller-Couch and her daughter generally met him on his arrival in London. The family stayed a few days in a service flat at Queen Anne's Mansions, while Q attended the annual meeting of the Imperial Society of Knights Bachelor and other functions and the ladies did some shopping.

When Q left home each term the railway officials at Par (the junction for Fowey) always gave him the same quasi-royal reception as those at Cambridge. What is more remarkable is that, as travellers noticed, the officials at the great termini of Paddington and Liverpool Street, with their thousands of passengers, treated him in exactly the same way.

Q was seventy in the autumn of 1933. When he celebrated his birthday (as usual) with the Red Herrings, he said to them: 'I am a certifiable old man now', but in fact he was in better health than ten years before and his mind had never lost the freshness of youth.

CHAPTER X

THE SEPTUAGENARIAN (1933-43)

WITHIN a few months of his seventieth birthday Q resigned from the Cornwall Education Committee after thirty years' service and also from the office of county alderman that he had held almost as long; but he continued to be an active magistrate and to take the same prominent part in affairs at Fowey that he had taken for so many years. He could not bear to be away from Fowey on any occasion of national rejoicing, even if it fell during his University terms; and he was consequently there to help to organize the celebration of the Silver Jubilee of King George V in May 1935. Two years later he was there again in May for the Coronation of King George VI and he enjoyed the festivities as much as ever. The day's programme included a performance (with such few alterations as were necessary) of the children's masque that he had composed for the coronation of 1911. His time away from Cambridge during this term, he wrote, was 'all spent in organizing small coronation festivities in this small corner. "Shadows we are"—and yet what fun!' Increasing age made no difference to his enjoyment of life at Fowey. He organized the annual regatta and its accompanying festivities with as much zest as ever, and when he had turned seventy he would still ride the wooden horses on the roundabouts at the fair held after the regatta.

He was much gratified when, in 1936, he was made a Freeman of his native Bodmin and greeted as the recognized spokesman of the Cornish people 'wherever Cornishmen are gathered together, in whatever part of the earth'. The day's ceremony carried his mind back sixty or more years, he said, to an occasion when he had taken part in beating the bounds of Bodmin and, as boys will, had fancied himself a Freeman of the borough already.

Fowey followed Bodmin's example by conferring its freedom on Q in September 1937 'in appreciation and acknowledgment of his eminent services to the borough and county, his great achievement in literature, and as an expression of the high esteem in which he is held by the Corporation and burgesses of the borough'. Q, in accepting the freedom, said that if in more than fifty years he had not taken liberties enough with Fowey he was puzzled to guess for what unbridled conduct in his old age the honour conferred on him gave him a blank cheque, so to speak. He recalled his first visit to Fowey when, as a boy of fifteen, he had resolved that he would make the town his home if he could; and he recalled his and Cardinal Newman's old rooms at Oxford, and the snapdragon growing on the wall there, which Newman had always accepted as an emblem of his own perpetual residence at Oxford, even unto death. 'My emblem', said Q, 'shall be a more common flower; you may almost call it a weed. It grows along the waterside here and refuses to be uprooted from the crevices of the sea wall. It is commonly known as pink valerian, but we call it the Pride of Fowey.'

On this same occasion the Mayor of Fowey (Colonel Edward Treffry, the son of the first mayor under the revived charter) informed the company that Q had accepted the unanimous invitation of the Borough Council to become their next mayor. It was most fitting, he said, that Q should hold the office; for he had made the Mayor of Troy famous in fiction and would make him even more famous in fact.

A few days later Q wrote to H. F. Stewart:

The Mayor-elect of Fowey presents his compliments to the University of Cambridge and proposes to return to it on October 9th or before, where he will carry on business as usual and hopes for a continuance of past favours. Your prayers, however, are earnestly desired.

When Treffry (our present mayor) came to me about this I gave in only on condition of having an energetic deputy, and propose to be absent from Cambridge but one week between beginning and end of term—for mayor-choosing on the statutory November 9th and church-parade on the following Sunday. (So now Dogberry will have 'two gowns and everything handsome about him'.) For that week I can double my classes if they clamour: and I propose two public lectures,

one of which I am now finishing: this on *Troilus and Cressida*, a
bad play of which I maintain hardily that not even a Shakespeare can
play the fool *understandingly* with classical matter in default of proper
baptism. . . .

Yours as ever

QUAGBERRY.

Q was duly installed as Mayor of Fowey on 9 November 1937.
He thoroughly enjoyed his year of office and Fowey enjoyed it too.
As he walked along the narrow street of the diminutive borough—
whether to Mr Rickard the barber for his morning shave, to the
Town Hall to discuss business with the Town Clerk, or to the
Yacht Club to choose the prizes or the music for the regatta—he
was greeted all the way and stopped every few yards to speak to
someone or other. They were people of every walk of life—the
originals, no doubt (or more usually the descendants of the
originals) of Nicky Vro, Caleb Trotter, Simon Colliver, or
Miss Marty. Whoever they were, he treated them all with the same
grave courtesy, and their attitude to him was deferential without
being in the least servile. According to the degree of their intimacy
with him, some addressed him as plain 'sir', some as 'Sir Arthur',
some as 'Q', some as 'Your Worship'. No visitor would have
been surprised to hear him addressed as 'Your Majesty', for Fowey
seemed to be a miniature kingdom and Q its king. Only a Béranger
could have done justice to the relationship between the two.
Everyone he met knew him and he knew everyone except the
holiday-makers who clicked their cameras as he went by and called
at The Haven during meal-times to ask him to sign copies of *Troy
Town*, *The Mayor of Troy*, or *The Delectable Duchy*.

Before his term of office as mayor was over Fowey celebrated
the silver jubilee of its return to borough status. As at the celebration of royal jubilees and coronations, there were peals of bells and
thanksgiving services at the parish church, a military display, teas
for the children and the elderly, and a fancy dress ball to wind up
the day. There was also a gathering at Place, under the tree where
the charter had been handed over in 1913; and Q, now Mayor of
Fowey, summarized the history of the twenty-five years which had

passed since then—years during which, he said, 'the old ship of Fowey has contrived to run on an even keel—a mere cockboat, to be sure, of the King's realm, yet sharing that wind of God's grace for which we gave thanks this morning'.

During his mayoralty he received the freedom of a third Cornish borough—the City of Truro. On this occasion, in addition to the usual parchment scroll recording his freedom, he was presented with a portrait of himself painted by Mr Henry Lamb, for which a number of his Cornish friends and admirers had subscribed. The portrait, which he in turn presented to the Royal Institution of Cornwall at Truro, showed him in informal dress—in lounge suit and raincoat, with a cloth cap in one hand and a pipe in the other.

His portrait had been painted at Cambridge four years previously by Mr (afterwards Sir) William Nicholson for the Roosters. This, like Mr Lamb's portrait, showed Q in informal dress—in one of his brightly coloured jackets and bow tie, holding the celebrated pen with which all his books had been written. Most of the sittings were in 'my dining room': hence the unusual red background of the portrait.

At Cambridge he was in as great demand as ever at both senior and junior functions. He seemed to become more and more fond of undergraduate company as he grew older. Among Roosters he was now often described by the title that had been conferred on him when he was made a Bard of the Cornish Gorsedd in 1928— 'the Red Knight'; and when another Fellow of the College, Sir Herbert Richmond (afterwards Master of Downing), who had been an admiral, became a Rooster in 1935 he was given the complementary title of 'the Blue Knight'. Q widened his circle of undergraduate friends when he became President of the University Whip Club, founded in 1938 'to encourage the sport and art of driving and to further the more general use of the horse'. He enjoyed driving out in a trap to a club lunch in some neighbouring village in company with Bernard Manning, who also held office in the club.

After he had turned seventy he declined more and more invitations to speak at meetings away from Cambridge during term but

Q, from the Portrait by Henry Lamb 1938

he declined by no means all of them. He went, for instance, to Oxford to lecture, to Horsham to unveil a memorial to Charles Lamb at Christ's Hospital, to Harrow School and Newport Grammar School in Essex to deliver speeches, and to London to address the Cornish Association, to give broadcast talks, or to preside over meetings of the newly founded Charles Lamb Society. When he and his family were making one of their end-of-term stays in London in 1937 they renewed their old friendship with J. M. Barrie. Barrie died in the same year and Q wrote to Sir Sydney Cockerell afterwards:

The best of our intimacy belonged to the early days, when e.g. he spent some weeks of his honeymoon at Fowey and I listened to his ambitions. As time went on and success came and distance separated us, naturally the confidences grew rarer as his self-confidence grew. Also he felt that I didn't like—I never do—the people of the theatre and their company 'off the stage': and also, again, he had an inkling that I thought the domestic crash—or the blame of it—was not all on one side. He never spoke to me of it, and I never alluded to it, of course. But his pretty frequent visits to Fowey came to an end. Recollections, no doubt.

For all that, our affection held, unstrained, to the end. A few months before his death he dined with us at Queen Anne's Mansions and talked away till past midnight—loth to go then, as he told us, rather wistfully.

Q's last volume of collected lectures and essays, called *The Poet as Citizen, and Other Papers*, was published in 1934. Most of its contents were originally delivered as lectures at Cambridge. One of them, 'Tradition and Orthodoxy', was a reply to Mr T. S. Eliot, who, with the ardour of an American convert to Toryism and Anglo-Catholicism, used the phrase, 'a society like ours, worm-eaten with Liberalism'. This roused Q, whose roots ran as deep into English tradition as they did into Liberalism and Anglicanism, and he replied:

What he means by 'Liberalism', except that it is something he dislikes, one must use patience to discern, so dexterously he shuffles religion into politics, politics into literature, tradition into dogma, to and fro, until the reader—let alone a listener—can scarcely tell out of which category the card (so to speak) is being dealt. Still if one keeps gripping, as Menelaus and his comrades did upon the Old Man of the Sea, this may be squeezed out—that 'Liberalism' is anything which questions dogma: which dogma, to be right dogma, is the priestly utterance of a particular offset of a particular branch of a historically fissiparous Church.

After tracing the tradition of Liberty throughout the history of English literature, he continued:

If we read the story aright, this 'Liberalism' which Mr Eliot arraigns as a worm, eating into the traditions of our society, reveals itself rather as Tradition itself, throughout Literature (which is Thought worth setting down and recording), the organic spirit persisting, aërating, preserving, the liberties our ancestors won and we inherit.

He concluded:

What is the alternative? What the dirty trump card ever up dogma's sleeve to be slid down and sneaked, upon opportunity? It is suppression; tyranny (as Pascal defined it, 'the determination to get in that way what you cannot in another'); in its final brutal word—force. Look around Europe to-day and consider under what masks dogma is not feeling for, or openly shaking, this weapon to cow the minds of free men; and ask yourselves if it be not the inherited duty of our race to vindicate the tradition of that Liberty which was the ark within the citadel of our father's souls.

After the publication of *The Poet as Citizen* Q turned again to the writing of his *Castle d'Or*, which he had laid aside for some years, to the writing of a book of reminiscences, and to the preparation of a new edition of *The Oxford Book of English Verse*. The reminiscences, like *Castle d'Or*, were left unfinished when he died, but the new *Oxford Book of English Verse* was published in November 1939.

It differed considerably from the book of 1900, for he had ejected about one hundred of the original selection of poems, added two hundred new ones, and extended the period of his anthology down to Armistice Day 1918. Even then, he said in his preface, he had admitted 'a few later numbers by poets who, whether consciously or not, had indicated before that date the trend of their genius', but he had not been able to trust his judgement of post-war poetry any further than that. This did not mean that he despised the younger generation of poets. On the contrary, he said:

Although I cannot dispute against Time, this is not to admit a charge of crabbed age: since it has been my good fortune to spend the most part of these later years with the young and to share—even in some measure to encourage—their zest for experiment. The Muses' house has many mansions: their hospitality has outlived many policies of State, more than a few religions, countless heresies—*tamen usque recurret Apollo*—and it were profane to misdoubt the Nine as having forsaken these so long favoured islands.

There were nevertheless those whom he did condemn, and he continued:

Of experiment I still hold myself fairly competent to judge. But, writing in 1939, I am at a loss what to do with a fashion of morose disparagement; of sneering at things long by catholic consent accounted beautiful; of scorning at 'Man's unconquerable mind' and hanging up (without benefit of laundry) our common humanity as a rag on a clothesline.

In some of the alterations that he made in the *Oxford Book* Q stands open to a charge of bowing the knee to Baal. For instance, he included poems by G. M. Hopkins, whom he did not like and whom he described in a letter during the following year as 'a precious, priestly, hot-house darling with (to my mind) no ear but a thumb'. In any event, he was running a grave risk by making any changes at all, for *The Oxford Book of English Verse* had long since become a classic of English literature. The significance of the year 1900, moreover, could never disappear, because a year that marks the end of any century is, whether it deserves it or not, inevitably a landmark in human history. The importance of the year 1918, on the other hand, which still seemed great even when Q wrote his preface at Whitsun 1939, slumped considerably with the outbreak of the second World War in the following September.

As in 1914, Q was at Fowey when the war began. Some weeks later he wrote to his friends, the Misses Nixon:

I have been kept here by various duties, Fowey having become for the nonce a 'garrison town' with a bewildering number of units scattered around—R.F.A., R.A.F., R.E., some Yeomanry, half a line battalion, not to mention the Navy—and myself the one handy J.P. sitting and representing Peace in the centre of the small cyclone. But I propose to get away to Cambridge on Wednesday. My rooms, I understand, are not disturbed, though the College, too, harbours a number of strange guests....

A German broadcast, the other day, announced that Fowey was in flames. Which it ain't, and hasn't been. Dr Goebbels must have heard of Troy, for the first time, and got the story mixed up.

Glad you thought *Hetty* passable. The story is well 'documented' any way; and if you are good you shall have a copy at Christmas—or no! I think you shall have *Sir John Constantine* (my favourite, and therefore the most *un*popular of the lot).

The 'strange guests' at Jesus College to whom he referred in this letter were members of the Royal Air Force, who occupied part of the College buildings until the spring of 1945. The rest of the buildings, however, were left untouched throughout the war, and the Government's policy of continuing the education of potential officers before and even during their military service was such that the number of undergraduates at the College never fell much below a hundred at any time. Few of them stayed the normal three years, and many stayed only six months; but there was no such break in the corporate life of the College as there had been during the war of 1914–18. Q did all he could to ensure that the undergraduates should lose as little University life as possible on account of the war. Consequently, when the University Pitt Club, to which he had belonged for a number of years, decided to close down for the duration of the war, he helped to found the Interim Club as a temporary substitute and accepted the office of president.

In January 1940, when he was on the very point of leaving home for Cambridge, he slipped on the frozen ground, injured himself rather severely, and had to spend a week in bed. He wrote to Cambridge to say that he was

reading Scott most of the day—yards of him: not as in the hot days of youth, of course, but with just as great though a quite different delight: and with awe, too. The stature of it all, and the catholic understanding of men and their affairs! And then I pick up this week's *New Statesman* and come on a sneering article by that precious lady, Virginia Woolf, all in the Lytton Strachey style of detraction. 'Gas at Abbotsford', she calls it. All the little selected details and hints to build the disparaging picture—and then a phrase escapes that gives the lady away—'Sir Walter himself, prosing and pompous'. Scott 'pompous'—good Lord!

Which is your favourite? I used to put *Old Mortality* first, with *The Antiquary* close up. Now this latter goes well down my list, and *Heart of Midlothian* heads it well, with *Mortality*, *Rob Roy* (yes, even so) and *Redgauntlet* in a bunch for second place.

This is the first letter I've attempted for these ten days. I intend to make for Cambridge as soon as my legs will carry me the length of Paddington platform. The pity is they didn't stand the cold as have the domestic waterpipes, which have behaved nobly through frost and thaw.

He arrived very late at Cambridge that term, but the discomforts and difficulties of war-time travel never caused him to miss a term altogether. In the summer term of 1940 he took part in the election of a new Master of Jesus College in succession to Arthur Gray, who had died during the Easter vacation at the age of eighty-seven. The military disasters of the early summer of that year did not alarm him in the least: he never at any time had the slightest doubt about the ultimate success of the allied cause. When air attacks began in earnest he used the College shelters at first and sitting there helped to solve cross-word puzzles or entertained the rest of the company by telling stories; but after two or three nights no air-raid siren ever induced him to leave his bed again, even when bombs were falling on Cambridge.

In August 1940, when he was at home for the vacation, he had a narrow escape in an air-raid on Fowey. In an account of it to a friend later he said:

We are all well here, by the mercy of Heaven and no thanks to the Boche. You haven't heard that the scoundrel dropped four heavy bombs on me the other day as I was working in my little orchard. No. 1 was a close call, striking the cliff some twenty feet from me and by the Lord's guidance sending the shards straight up, to scatter high over me as I fell on my face. No. 2 tore down a cantle of cliff, blasted a couple of oaks, 'incidentally' (as the journalists say) removing a crow's nest into the *Ewigkeit*. No. 3 made a large crater, destroyed a neat brake, dispersed the shale underneath it for some fifty yards. No. 4 fell harmlessly into the sea. So, you see, we live in what the Government calls a 'protected area'. We have had a field or two ploughed up with smaller bombs at the back of us, a schoolhouse (empty) broken, with some cottages in Polruan. But we go about our business, surrounded by the navy and army in numbers, with cannon to right of us, ditto to left of us—a Bren gun in the next garden, for one. And we are picking in a tolerable crop of apples and pears, with a bumper crop of plums and bullaces (why are plums so prolific this year? Chivers may know, who supplies the Forces). And now, to my joy, the wind is S.W. after this long drought, and knocking up quite a sea in the Channel. My wife (who always and instinctively drives at practice) suggests that if the Germans try to invade to-night they will be horribly sea-sick....

This vacation has somehow been as empty for me as if by illness. Actually the house has been crowded with relatives of whom I am fond —with a young schoolboy to keep us all active and slam every door he doesn't leave open. But *noise* has everywhere invaded this haven— speed-boat on patrol, gun-practice, siren-warnings, bombs, military cyclists hurrying in to buy a postage stamp: truth, I suspect, is that although I felt no ill effects at the time of my little shock the explosions (which seemed to join in one and were really terrific) have played a bit on the aural nerves, so that I find myself jumping at any bang of a door (and everybody bangs doors nowadays: result of slamming doors of cars). I must cure myself of this, but it's abominably difficult to sit down to *work*.

There were further air attacks on Fowey in 1941 and Q wrote to the Misses Nixon from Jesus College in October:

Yes, of course I'm the World's Worst Correspondent. Didn't you know it?

In answer to kind enquiries—Fowey, by latest advice, stands where it did. Only two other bombings—one of which smashed an Elementary School-house (out of school hours) and t'other set fire to a hayrick. The small harbour now bristles with guns and other defences. But invasion seems to be off the programme. For this I have a sneaking regret: because *if* the nasty fellow had attempted it (he knowing nothing of the sea) he'd have met with a disaster to make future readers of history shudder—a massacre so awful that, as a decently humane fellow, I'm rather glad he funked it. . . .

I travelled here via Oxford, where quiet has reigned. My old friends at the 'Randolph' found me a room, though the place is packed. Also my old College offered me quarters. Cambridge is livelier with a raid warning now and then, and protective planes droning overhead a good part of the time.

This description of himself as 'the World's Worst Correspondent' was typical of Q. 'Try', he wrote to Lord Alfred Douglas in 1943, 'to forgive a friend to whom letter-writing has been the very devil all through a long life. I love actual talk and can claim to be quite a good listener, but the world's worst correspondent.'

In these self-accusations he did himself less than justice. It is true that he often delayed answering letters; but that was inevitable, for he was (as he often emphasized) a slow writer, he rarely employed secretarial help, and his mail was generally a big one. In addition to letters concerned with University affairs at Cambridge and magisterial and other public business at Fowey it included numerous letters from friends and from readers of his books; literary queries; letters that pretended to be from serious seekers after literary truth but were in fact thinly disguised attempts to get his help in solving crossword puzzles; invitations to make speeches, to open buildings, to distribute prizes, or to judge competitions; and requests from complete strangers to write Introductions to their books, to write essays, verses, plays, or stories (free of charge) for their pet charities, or to criticize their poems—varying in length from a sonnet to an epic. He answered them all (or nearly all) sooner or later, even though he was on occasion moved to refer to their writers as 'those devils', and even though once (just before the war began) when he was told that Secret Service agents were opening and reading people's letters he remarked: 'They are welcome to read all mine—provided they answer them.' If any of his friends or neighbours went through a difficult time or suffered a family bereavement no one was quicker than he in writing to express sympathy. He wrote beautiful letters of condolence, as is shown by the following example, which he sent from Cambridge to a small tradesman at Fowey whose wife had died:

Dear Mr ——,

I have just heard this sad news, and I want to tell you—and am commissioned to say—how sorry at The Haven we all are.

In the old days my wife and I, coming away from the Armoury, often told one another what a pleasure it was to see you two dancing together and often—ourselves happily married—wished that your evident happiness might hold in devotion all your days. Her days were short, but I know how truly the devotion lasted. She was always gracious to me; and (if I may say it) her face had for her friends a particular beauty.

Do not answer this. I hope to be at home again in less than a month. But I must write to tell you that an old friend wants to send a word just now.

Yours sincerely,
ARTHUR QUILLER-COUCH.

In December 1941, just after Q had returned to Fowey for the Christmas vacation, Jesus College suffered a great loss by the death of its Senior Tutor, Bernard Manning. He was thirty years younger than Q, but they had been very close friends and Q felt his death keenly. When he heard the news he wrote from Fowey, 'I had no idea, when Manning and I parted at the Evelyn Nursing Home with the usual Christmas wishes, that he was in any serious —or, rather, immediate—danger, and the Master's telegram fairly stunned me. You won't want me to tell you of my affection for one who was the best of our friends and the one whose loss must mean such a blow to the College that one never thought of anything so unthinkable.'

Q and Bernard Manning had for years made a point of lunching together at the Pitt Club on Sundays during term. When the war began and the club ceased to function, Jesus College obtained a lease of the premises and served lunch there every day for its members, because the College Hall during the earlier years of the war was monopolized by the Air Force in the middle part of the day. Consequently Q could now be seen walking along Jesus Lane to lunch at the Pitt almost every day of the week. In the spring of 1942, however, the Ministry of Food commandeered the premises for use as a British Restaurant for the general public and advertised a tenpenny lunch there. On the spur of the moment Q wrote:

> Though our Club has had notice to quit,
> Yet as Britons we still claim admittance;
> So our last one-and-eightpence we'll split
> And we'll feast at the Pitt for a pittance.

He never once, however, exercised his British privilege; a re-arrangement of Air Force hours of duty enabled him to lunch at Jesus College again.

The College had always had undisturbed possession of the Hall in the evenings and in November that year the Roosters held their annual dinner in it on Q's seventy-ninth birthday. When he replied to the toast of his health he described himself as 'a period piece, but not yet a museum piece'. A few days later he lectured on 'The Problem of *Timon*', which he considered 'no play at all'. 'I wonder', he wrote to a friend, 'why the idolaters keep consider-ing Shakespeare as a static artist? Did ever—could ever—a really great artist grow without a number of mistakes, bad shots, unhappy failures? *I* know that I reverence all the better, and hope to under-stand him the better, for separating his great work from his misfits.'

That appears to have been the last of his formal lectures for the English Tripos, though he continued with his Aristotle classes and also gave some informal lectures outside the University. His post-bag was still a full one and in the Easter vacation of 1943 he wrote that he had just arrived at Fowey from Cambridge, 'hotly pursued by parcels of bad verse'. In April he addressed an audience of members of the Forces at Cambridge on 'Modest Ignorance'—'in which, as you know', he wrote to a friend, 'I am something of an expert'. In September he wrote from Fowey, 'I have been shamefully idle in writing—and in everything for that matter except in bodily toil, helping the war effort as far as an old man may, with bill-hook, saw and other implements, in clearing land and storing timber.' In November he cut his Cambridge term short in order to be at Fowey for his eightieth birthday. When he heard that someone had remarked: 'Many people forget that Q still exists,' he raised a warning finger and whispered: ''Sh! he's dead—but he doesn't want it generally known.'

CHAPTER XI

LAST DAYS (1943-44)

Q'S eightieth birthday produced many tributes to him in the newspapers as the doyen of English men of letters and brought him several hundreds of letters of congratulation. 'For two or three days', he wrote, 'it snowed a blizzard of letters and telegrams. Beneath the pile of it I felt—I, the world's worst correspondent—much like an old sheep who lets the snowstorm cover her, snuggles down in the hollow warmed by her own body and quietly sleeps her last.' One newspaper, he said, 'sent down a camera-man, with the notion of putting me into its Christmas Number, and the fellow hounded me about so cruelly that it strained my heart and I had to take to my bed for a bit'.

While he was recuperating he spent a good deal of his time writing letters. One of them was to Lord Alfred Douglas, who during the autumn had delivered a lecture on 'The Principles of Poetry' to the Royal Society of Literature. 'I "purred"', Q wrote to him, 'over your address and again over your news that the hearers took it with joy. Indeed there are signs—even in poor old Cambridge—that sensible people are sickening of the T. S. Eliot game (Has he ever written three consecutive lines of poetry in his life?) of perpetually "debunking" beauty and sneering at it.'

Q was up and about again before Christmas and was able to take part in decorating the house on Christmas Eve—a ceremony in which he always delighted. As in previous years, he provided a Christmas tree for his grand-nephew, Guy Symondson, who with his mother had made his home at The Haven while his father was away on war service. He was now at a public school and had grown out of such things as Christmas trees, but Q was glad to use him as an excuse for his own devotion to the festival. As always, he spent part of the afternoon of Christmas Day reading Hans Andersen.

When he returned to Cambridge in January 1944 his brain was as clear and his judgement as sound as ever. Age had bent him a little, so that he did not look his five feet ten inches in height. He was as slim as he had always been. His red hair had long since turned white but showed no sign of baldness. He had for years taken to clipping his once luxuriant moustache very close, so that from a few yards away he seemed to be clean-shaven. The deep furrow down each side of his mouth was not a sign of age: it had always been there, and he had in fact inherited it from his mother, as photographs taken at the time of her marriage show. His features, though rough-hewn, had few wrinkles and he possessed the clear, healthy complexion of an undergraduate.

He had preserved a few provincialisms in his speech—West Country expressions—all through life. They were very few and amounted to little more than pronouncing the vowel in the word *food* short (as in *foot*), to sounding the *l* in *almond* and to sounding only one *n* in *penknife*. He did not carry into his speech those few mannerisms that are to be found in his writings—the use of such expressions as *a plenty*, *the most*, *the both*, the use of the verb *miss* where other people put *fail* ('He missed to notice') and the excessive use of the subjunctive. He did, however, use a few dialect words, such as *carneying*. Once, when asked to explain the meaning of this word, he said: 'Well, take —. She's a carneying person. She comes to me washing her hands in invisible soap and saying: "Oh no, Sir Arthur, I can't do enough for you, Sir Arthur"; and, to do her justice, she doesn't.'

At the age of eighty he still began every day at Cambridge with a tepid bath in an icy bathroom. Having finished his bath he dressed for the morning—without hurrying; for dressing was to him, like everything he did, a ceremony that had to be carried out properly. No one ever succeeded in making him rush through anything unnecessarily, though if speed was essential he would be as quick as anyone. Always the best-dressed man in Cambridge, he was so still. If he was to deliver a formal lecture during the morning he put on correct morning dress. Otherwise he put on either a tweed suit of brighter colours than most men dared to wear or a bright brown jacket and shooting breeches, with stockings and high spats. Whatever else he wore, he would have a silk handkerchief (of a colour to match his suit) in his breast pocket and would wear a stiff double collar, and a blue or brown bow tie sown with fairly large white roundels. The corners of his jackets were always cut square, never rounded off.

The next ceremony was breakfast, which he took at the side table in his keeping room. Although he was always very particular about the selection, the cooking and the serving of food, he ate remarkably little at this or any other meal. After breakfast he wrote a letter home: throughout fifty-four years of married life he had written home every day whenever he was away. He then dealt with his ordinary correspondence and with literary work until lunch-time. If he had no meetings or calls to pay out of college during the afternoon, he often changed just before lunch into riding-breeches and leggings—sometimes (during the summer) into white yachting trousers and blue reefer jacket.

Unless he was lunching out of College or entertaining a party in the Guest Room he lunched in Hall. He liked everyone else lunching at high table to go to his rooms afterwards for a drink and a smoke. Here he either sat among his guests or (if any topic requiring close thought came under discussion) would walk very slowly up and down the room with his hands clasped behind his back. When his guests had gone, if he had no meeting of the Faculty Board of English or any similar body to attend, he would read or doze awhile in his cane-bottomed chair beside the fire, or stroll on to the Close to watch a match or occasionally go to the College boat-house to see the boats coming and going.

After taking tea in his rooms or at a café or at the Interim Club he would settle down again to reading and writing. Shortly before seven o'clock he would change into a dark suit, regretting meanwhile that dons did not dine in proper evening dress nowadays. At half-past seven he would go to dinner in Hall, setting his jaw very firmly if the undergraduate who read the Latin grace was guilty of a false quantity. Unless he had an engagement to keep after dinner or was in the throes of preparing a lecture he would sit for some time in the Combination Room, smoking and entertaining the company with his wit and humour. When he had returned to his rooms, to which he invited someone or other almost every evening, a very little persuasion would induce him to talk of his past intimates—of Charles Cannan, Robert Bridges, Thomas Hardy, Kenneth Grahame, J. M. Barrie, or Charles Whibley, who had been an Honorary Fellow of the College from 1912 until his death in 1930. He would talk, too, on such favourite topics as rowing, gardening, and Fowey—perhaps most of all about Fowey. He would often express his regret that he had not been given a free hand with the Fellows' garden, which he used to say he would have converted into a paradise.

When his guests had gone he would devote himself again to work until bedtime. He liked to have company while undressing —an operation that he performed from below upwards. As he took off each garment he folded it carefully and carried it into his bedroom, talking all the time. His undressing was a miniature drama, with entrances, exits, speeches, and now and then a hoarse stage-whisper from behind the scenes when he dropped a stud or jabbed his toe against a piece of furniture. If he had been out to a feast he looked a particularly strange sight when he stood barefoot but otherwise in complete evening dress; stranger still when, having disappeared into the wings to put away his trousers, he reappeared and stood framed in the doorway of his bedroom— bare-legged, with shirt-tails hanging down under his white waistcoat and tail coat. When he had got into his pyjamas he sat down by the fire for a last cigarette and then dismissed his guest. Within a very few minutes of getting into bed he was fast asleep under a copy of John Speed's map of Cornwall, with its dolphins blowing full-rigged ships along the English Channel home to Fowey.

His life at Cambridge during the earlier part of the Lent term of 1944 followed the familiar routine but it soon became clear that he was out of sorts. The weather was severe and he seemed to feel it more than he had ever been known to do. He had trouble too with his jaw and found difficulty in feeding and in holding a pipe in his mouth. As the term wore on he became more and more unwell and on 1 March he left Cambridge for Fowey, where he started on a course of medical treatment. For a time his health improved and he was able to preside over the annual meeting of the Fowey Cottage Hospital and fulfil other public engagements. On 23 March, when taking his usual morning walk to the Yacht Club, he stepped out of the way of a passing car, stumbled over the kerb-stone and fell down. He cut his face and was badly shaken but not seriously injured. His health, nevertheless, deteriorated rapidly in April and before the month was out he had to take to his bed. Although he felt too weak to write letters his life-long optimism did not desert him. On 4 May he dictated a letter to be sent to Jesus College, saying that he hoped to be back in residence in June; but on 12 May, when Fowey and the country for miles round were packed with troops and the harbour and its inlets with ships, all waiting in a tense silence for the signal to invade France, he died.

Three days later six naval men carried his coffin into the parish church where he had been married and his children christened and where he had so often worshipped and read the Lessons. Behind the coffin walked his boatman-gardener, Joseph Welch, carrying a bunch of pink valerian. Next came the family mourners and after them a great company of people. They were of every occupation and rank, as befitted the funeral of one who had served his fellows without regard to class and maintained that 'an artist exists to serve his art and his art to serve men and women'. He was buried in the cemetery on the hillside above the little town that he had loved so well.

Q has many claims to be remembered by posterity. Those who knew him personally will remember him as an original character, a humorist, an entertaining conversationalist, a charming and generous host, and a friend of all who turned to him in any kind of trouble. A far wider circle will remember him as a writer of beautiful, chaste English prose who (to quote the memorial tablet in Truro Cathedral) 'as author, critic and anthologist kindled in others a lively and discriminating love of English literature'; and he will be remembered as a great Cornishman.

It would have been unfitting if he had died anywhere but in Cornwall, for he loved the county of his birth so much, absorbed its spirit so fully and wrote about it so extensively that his name and the name of Cornwall can never be separated.

Yet his was no narrow county feeling. His devotion to Cornwall was in fact the foundation of an equal devotion to his country. He loved the history, the scenery, the institutions and the people of England as much as he loved its language and its literature, even though it was for his devotion to these last two that his name became known throughout the world.

Neither was his patriotism a narrow one. The charges of insularity and jingoism, which are so frequently brought against the men of the Victorian age, could not be justly brought against him, for no one believed more firmly than he in the fundamental decency of the human race as a whole. That belief is implicit in practically everything he wrote, from first to last. He did not, as so many do, allow his faith in human goodness to slip away from him as he grew old. That was why he championed humanity to the end against the 'debunking' school of writers, who seemed to him to take a delight in slandering the dead and in jeering at the ordinary decencies of life.

The essential difference between him and most of the 'debunkers' was that he believed in the spiritual world while they believed in practically nothing—scarcely, one might say, even in themselves. He stated this difference, and its effect on literary output, long before the word 'debunking' reached England. Speaking of himself and like-minded people in his book of essays, *From a Cornish Window*, he said:

We agree—at least I assume this—that men have souls as well as intellects, that above and beyond the life we know and can describe and reduce to laws and formulas there exists a spiritual life of which our intellect is unable to render account. We have (it is believed) affinity with this spiritual world, and we hold it by virtue of something spiritual within us, which we call the soul. You may disbelieve in this spiritual region and remain, I dare say, an estimable citizen; but I cannot see what business you have with poetry, or what satisfaction you draw from it. Nay, poetry demands that you believe in something further; which is, that in this spiritual region resides and is laid up that eternal scheme of things, that universal order, of which the phenomena of this world are but fragments, if indeed they are not mere shadows.

Q's steadfast championship of humanity and the spiritual world in an age when both were being repeatedly attacked was the inevitable outcome of his chivalrous nature. It is a significant fact that his own favourite among all his novels was *Sir John Constantine*, the hero of which is a Cornish knight-errant of the eighteenth century. 'If', he says in his preface, 'you would know anything of the writer who has so often addressed you under an initial, you may find as much of him here as in any of his books'; and anyone who knew Q can scarcely fail to see that in Sir John Constantine he drew a portrait of himself as he would have liked to be.

No more appropriate honour could have been conferred on him than the knighthood that he received in 1910. Consciously or unconsciously, he was actuated all his life by the principles of knighthood as they had been laid down by medieval theorists, even if theory in the Middle Ages remained untranslated into fact as often as not—the principles, that is to say, of loyalty, of courtesy, of defending the right, of helping the weak and the oppressed. Those who knew him can recall numerous instances of his quiet but life-long devotion to these principles. Others can find it scattered throughout his writings. It runs, for instance, right through *Major Vigoureux*, through his *Memories and Opinions*, and through innumerable short stories, such as *The Spinster's Maying*, *The Paupers*, *Colonel Baigent's Christmas*, and *Corporal Sam*. His chivalrous heroes are frequently poor people. That was characteristic of Q: he was not one of those who imagine that chivalry cannot exist apart from money or high social position. None of his characters has more of the knight-errant in him than the unlettered Corporal Sam, who knowingly throws away his life to avenge the honour of a poor Spanish woman whom he had never seen alive.

In nothing was Q's chivalry more evident than in his attitude towards women—again, both in real life and in his writings, whether one considers his critical works or his fiction. No fewer than four of his novels—*Lady Good-for-Nothing, Ia, Hetty Wesley* and *The Westcotes*—might well have as their sub-title, *A Defence of a Woman*; and probably no other literary critic has gone out of his way to break a lance with W. S. Gilbert for 'exposing women to public derision on the stage just because they are growing old and losing their beauty', as he put it in one of his lectures.

The hero of one of his novels utters these words as he lies dying:

Learn of me that love, though it delight in youth, yet forsakes not the old; nay, though through life its servant follow and never overtake....

You will need to trust it, for it will change. Lose no faith in the beam when, breaking from your lady's eyes, it fires you not as before. It widens; it is not slackening; it is passing, enlarging into a diviner light. By that light you shall see all men, women, children—yes, and all living things—akin with you and deserving your help. It is the light of God upon earth, and its warmth is God's charity, though He kindle it first as a selfish spark between a youth and a maid.

Trust it, then, most of all when it frightens you, its first passion fading. For then, sickening of what is transient, it dies to put on permanence; as the creature dies—as I am dying—into the greatness of the Creator....

O Master, who payest not by time, take the thanks of thy servant! O Captain, receive my sword! O hands, O wounded hands, reach and resume my soul! *In manus tuas, Domine—in manus—in manus tuas.*

Such were the last words of Sir John Constantine. They might equally well have been the last words of Sir Arthur Quiller-Couch.

Cujus animae propitietur Deus.

CHRONOLOGICAL LIST OF Q'S
PUBLICATIONS

including a selection from his contributions to periodical literature

a. Anthology.   *n.* Novel.

1881. *Athens, a Poem.* (Liddell and Son, Bodmin.)
1882. *Olympia, a Poem.* (Not published.)
1885–1943. Contributions to *The Oxford Magazine.*
1886. Edited *The Rattle,* vol. 1 (6 nos., 25 Feb.–3 March).
1887. *n.* *Dead Man's Rock.*
1888. *n.* *The Astonishing History of Troy Town.*
1889. *n.* *The Splendid Spur.*
       Edited *The World of Adventure, a Collection of Stirring Scenes and Moving Accidents,* 3 vols. 1889–91. (6 vols. of selections were published 1904–5, entitled *The Red, Green, Blue, Brown, Black,* and *Grey Adventure Books.*)
1890–99. Contributions to *The Speaker.*
1891. *n.* *The Blue Pavilions.*
       Noughts and Crosses: Stories, Studies, and Sketches.
1892. *The Warwickshire Avon,* with Illustrations by Alfred Parsons.
       I Saw Three Ships, and Other Winter's Tales.
       A Blot of Ink, translated from the French of René Bazin by Q and Paul M. Francke.
       Edited *The World of Romance, a Treasury of Tales, Legends, and Traditions.*
1893. *The Delectable Duchy: Stories, Studies, and Sketches.*
       Green Bays: Verses and Parodies. Cf. 1930.
       Introduction to *Verses by the Way,* by James Dryden Hosken.
       'My First Book.' (*The Idler,* pp. 47–60.)
1894. 'Troy Town Revisited.' (*The English Illustrated Magazine,* Oct., pp. 88–100.)
1895. *Wandering Heath: Stories, Studies, and Sketches.*
       Fairy Tales Far and Near Re-told, with Illustrations by H. R. Millar.
    a. *The Golden Pomp, a Procession of English Lyrics from Surrey to Shirley.*
       Edited *The Story of the Sea,* 2 vols. 1895–96.
1896. *n.* *Ia.*
       Poems and Ballads. Cf. 1929.
       Adventures in Criticism. (Articles reprinted from *The Speaker.*) 2nd edn, 1924 (several omissions).

1897. *a.*   *English Sonnets*, with Introduction and Notes. Cf. 1935.

1898.   Completed *St Ives*, by Robert Louis Stevenson.
         Edited *The Cornish Magazine*: vol. I, July–Dec. 1898; vol. II, Jan.–
         May 1899 (then discontinued).

1899. *n.*   *The Ship of Stars.*
         Historical Tales from Shakespeare.
         A Fowey Garland. (Light verse.)

1900.   *Old Fires and Profitable Ghosts: a Book of Stories.*
      a.   *The Oxford Book of English Verse* 1250–1900. Cf. 1939.

1901.   *The Laird's Luck and Other Fireside Tales.*

1902. *n.*   *The Westcotes.*
         The White Wolf and Other Fireside Tales.

1903. *n.*   *The Adventures of Harry Revel.*
      n.   *Hetty Wesley.*
         Two Sides of the Face: Midwinter Tales.

1904. *n.*   *Fort Amity.*
         Introduction to *Tennyson's Poems, a Selection*. ('Cassell's National
         Library.')

1905. *n.*   *Shining Ferry.*
         Shakespeare's Christmas and Other Stories.

1906. *n.*   *Sir John Constantine.*
      n.   *The Mayor of Troy.*
         From a Cornish Window. (Articles reprinted from *The Pall Mall
         Magazine*.)
      a.   *The Pilgrim's Way, a Little Scrip of Good Counsel for Travellers.* (Prose
         and verse.)
         Introduction to *Poems of Matthew Arnold* 1849–67. ('World's
         Classics.') Reprinted in *Studies in Literature*, 1918; also as Intro-
         duction to *The Poetical Works of Matthew Arnold* ('Oxford Poets')
         1942.

1907. *n.*   *Poison Island.*
      n.   *Major Vigoureux.*
         Merry-Garden and Other Stories.
         Introduction to *Eothen*, by A. W. Kinglake. ('Red Letter Library.')
         Introduction to *The Poems of Coleridge, a Selection*. ('World's Classics.')
         Reprinted in *Studies in Literature*, 1918.
         Introduction to *The Muse in Motley*, Verses by Hartley Carrick.

1908–12. Edited *Select English Classics*, with Introductions, 33 small volumes,
         viz. Early English Lyrics, Old Ballads, Robin Hood Ballads,
         Everyman, Marlowe, Shakespeare's Songs and Sonnets, Bacon,
         Jonson, Walton, Milton's Minor Poems, Marvell, Bunyan, Defoe,
         Seventeenth-Century 'Characters', Horace Walpole, Goldsmith,
         Cowper, Boswell, Crabbe, Blake, Wordsworth, Sonnets of Milton

and Wordsworth, Coleridge, Lamb, Hazlitt, Napier, Shelley, Keats, Hood, Tennyson, Browning, Whitman, Matthew Arnold.

1909. *n.* *True Tilda.*

Edited *Tennyson's Poems, a Selection*, with an Introduction. ('Little Classics.')

Introduction to *The Tempest*, by William Shakespeare. Illustrated by Edmund Dulac. (Undated: not later than 1909.)

1910. *n.* *Lady Good-for-Nothing.*

Corporal Sam and Other Stories.

The Sleeping Beauty and Other Fairy Tales from the Old French Retold. Illustrated by Edmund Dulac.

a. *The Oxford Book of Ballads.*

'Thomas Edward Brown.' (*Encyclopædia Britannica*, 11th edn, iv. 662–3).

1911. *n.* *Brother Copas.*

This Royal Throne of Kings: a Children's Masque performed on the Coronation Day of King George V.

Edited *Pervigilium Veneris*, with Introduction. ('Oxford Plain Texts.')

1912. *n.* *Hocken and Hunken, a Tale of Troy.*

The Vigil of Venus and Other Poems. Reprinted in *Poems*, 1929.

The Roll Call of Honour, a New Book of Golden Deeds. (3 of the 10 chapters were reprinted 1925 as *Honourable Men* and 3 others 1926 as *Victors of Peace*.)

My Best Book. (3 short stories, 2 of them being reprints.)

a. *The Oxford Book of Victorian Verse.*

Introduction to *Parodies and Imitations Old and New*, edited by J. A. S. Adam and B. C. White.

'Three Open Letters to the Right Rev. Archibald Robertson, D.D., Lord Bishop of Exeter.' (*The Eye-Witness*, 1, 8, 15 Aug.)

1913–43. Contributions to *The Cambridge Review.*

1913. *News from the Duchy.* (Short stories and sketches, including *Tom Tiddler's Ground*, a sequel to *Major Vigoureux*.)

In Powder and Crinoline: Old Fairy Tales Retold. Illustrated by Kay Nielsen.

Introduction to *A Book of Pictures*, by Arthur Rackham.

Introduction to *Cambridge Poets 1900–1913*, an Anthology, edited by Aelfrida Tillyard.

'Voices on the Bank.' (*The Cambridge Review*, 4 June.)

1914. *Poetry.* ('Fellowship Books', edited by Mary Stratton.)

An Appeal to Cornishwomen, for the Cornwall Parliamentary Recruiting Committee.

Introduction to *Isabella*, by John Keats, edited by M. Robertson.

'Avuncular.' (98 lines of verse, *Chanticlere*, No. 64.)

1914.   'Charles Reade.' (*The Times Lit. Suppl.*) Reprinted in *Studies in Literature*, 1918.

1915. *n.*   *Nicky-Nan, Reservist.*
    'To the Front from the Backs.' (*The Cambridge Review*, 24 Feb.)

1916.   *On the Art of Writing: Lectures delivered in the University of Cambridge 1913–14.*
    The Mayor of Troy, a Play produced at the Haymarket Theatre 22 April–13 May. (Not printed.)

1917.   *Mortallone and Aunt Trinidad, Tales of the Spanish Main.*
    Memoir of Arthur John Butler.
    Introduction to *Characters of Shakespeare's Plays*, by W. Hazlitt. ('World's Classics.')
    Review of *Life of Swinburne*, by Edmund Gosse. (*The Edinburgh Review.*) Reprinted in *Studies in Literature*, 1918.

1918. *n.*   *Foe-Farrell.*
    Shakespeare's Workmanship.
    Studies in Literature. [1st Series.]
    '"And not as the Scribes", a Lay Address given in the Church of St Edward, Cambridge, 27 January.' (*The Cambridge Review*, 31 Jan.)

1919.   'Thoughts on University Reform.' (*The Cambridge Review*, 4 June.)

1920–44. General Editor of 'The King's Treasuries of Literature.'

1920.   *On the Art of Reading: Lectures delivered in the University of Cambridge 1916–1917 [sic, for 1916–18].*
    Introduction to *Selections from Coleridge's Biographia Literaria and from Wordsworth*, edited by G. Sampson.
    Introduction to *Poetry and Religion*, by Israel Abrahams.
    'Charles Cannan 1858–1919.' (*The Oxford Magazine*, 23 Jan.) Reprinted in *Memories and Opinions*, 1944, pp. 78–85.
    Obituary of Alastair Grahame. (*The Oxford Magazine*, 18 June.)
    Review of *Cambridge Poets 1914–20*, edited by E. L. Davison. (*The Cambridge Review*, 3 Dec.)

1921.   *Selected Stories, chosen by the Author.* ('The King's Treasuries of Literature.')
    The New Cambridge Edition of the Works of Shakespeare: The Comedies, edited for the Syndics of the Cambridge University Press by Q and J. Dover Wilson, with Introductions by Q, 14 vols., 1921–31, viz. 1921, *The Tempest, Merry Wives, Two Gentlemen of Verona*; 1922, *Measure for Measure, Comedy of Errors*; 1923, *Love's Labour's Lost, Much Ado*; 1924, *Midsummer Night's Dream*; 1926, *Merchant of Venice, As You Like It*; 1928, *Taming of the Shrew*; 1929, *All's Well That Ends Well*; 1930, *Twelfth Night*; 1931, *Winter's Tale*.
    Introduction to *Mice and Other Poems*, by Gerald Bullett.

1921.   Introduction to *A Book of Ships and Seamen*, by R. Wilson. ('The King's Treasuries of Literature.')

           Introduction to *The Cornish Handbook*, edited by John Kinsman.

           Edited *The Good-Natur'd Man*, by Oliver Goldsmith, with Introduction. ('Cambridge Plain Texts.')

           Edited *Sermons XV and LXVI*, by John Donne, with Introduction. ('Cambridge Plain Texts.')

1922.   *Studies in Literature*, 2nd Series.

           'Troilus and Cressida.' (*The Cambridge Review*, 10 March.)

           Obituary of Sir Walter Raleigh. (*The Cambridge Review*, 19 May.)

1923.   Obituary of Lewis Charles Foster. (*Western Morning News*, 13 Jan.)

           'A Lay Address given in the Church of All Saints, Cambridge, on 11 November.' (*All Saints Parish Magazine*, Dec.)

1924.   *The Children's Bible*, edited by A. Nairne, Q, and T. R. Glover.

           The Little Children's Bible, edited by A. Nairne, Q, and T. R. Glover.

           Contributed to *Byron, the Poet: a Collection of Addresses*, edited by W. A. Briscoe.

           'Anthony Trollope.' (*The Nation*, 3 and 10 May.) Reprinted in *Charles Dickens*, 1925.

1925.   *Charles Dickens and Other Victorians.*

    a.   *The Oxford Book of English Prose.*

           Introduction to *Cornish Granite, Extracts from the Writings and Speeches of Lord Courtney of Penwith.*

1926.   *The Age of Chaucer.* ('The Englishman.')

           Introduction to *The Wise Shepherd and Other Poems*, by Joseph Braddock.

1927.   *A Lecture on Lectures.* ('Hogarth Lectures on Literature', No. 1.)

           Introduction to *The Cornwall Education Week Handbook.*

           Introduction to *Pit-Head Poems*, by F. C. Boden.

           Obituary of Sir Sidney Colvin. (*The Cambridge Review*, 27 May.)

1928.   *The Cambridge Shorter Bible*, edited by A. Nairne, Q, and T. R. Glover.

           The Duchy Edition of Tales and Romances by Q (with new Introductions), 30 vols. 1928–29, viz. 1928, *Dead Man's Rock, Troy Town, Noughts and Crosses, Splendid Spur, Delectable Duchy, The Westcotes* with *Ia* and *Tom Tiddler's Ground, Blue Pavilions, Ship of Stars, Wandering Heath, Harry Revel, Hetty Wesley, Old Fires and Profitable Ghosts, Fort Amity, I Saw Three Ships* and *Mortallone, Sir John Constantine, Brother Copas, Laird's Luck, Shining Ferry, Mayor of Troy, Major Vigoureux, True Tilda, White Wolf, Poison Island, Lady Good-for-Nothing*; 1929, *Hocken and Hunken, News from the Duchy, Nicky-Nan, Foe-Farrell, Two Sides of the Face, Merry Garden.* (The volumes of short stories have a number of transferences and omissions.)

1928.   Introduction to *The Jesus College Boat Club, Cambridge*, by F. Brittain and H. B. Playford.

1929.   *Studies in Literature*, 3rd Series.

    Poems. (Contains all but 3 of the items in *Poems and Ballads* 1896, and the whole of *The Vigil of Venus and Other Poems* 1912, with 7 other items.)

    Review of *The Testament of Beauty*, by Robert Bridges. (*The Cambridge Review*, 29 Nov.)

1930.   *Green Bays: Verses and Parodies.* New and enlarged edition. (Contains 23 of the 27 items of 1893 edition + 11 other items.)

    Virgil: an Address to the Boys of Sevenoaks School. Privately printed.

    Edited *Thomas Edward Brown, a Memorial Volume 1830–1930*, with a Memoir by Q.

  a. *Pages of English Prose 1390–1930.* (A selection from *The Oxford Book of English Prose* 1925, with an Introduction to each excerpt and one new excerpt.)

    Introduction to *The Acts of the Apostles*.

    Introduction to *The Letters of Maarten Maartens*, edited by his daughter, Ada van der Poorten Schwartz.

    Introduction to *The Rime of the Ancient Mariner*, by S. T. Coleridge, designed by Bruce Rogers.

    Introduction to *Cornish Recipes Ancient and Modern*, compiled by Edith Martin, 5th edn.

1931.   Introduction to *Fairbairn of Jesus*, by Steve Fairbairn.

    Introduction to *South Mymms: the Story of a Parish*, by F. Brittain.

1932.   *Paternity in Shakespeare: Annual Shakespeare Lecture to the British Academy.* Reprinted in *The Poet as Citizen*, 1934.

    'Fifty Years: Books and Other Friends.' (*The Times*, 9 and 10 Feb.)

    Letter to the Editor of *The Times* on the death of Kenneth Grahame. (*The Times*, 14 July.)

1933.   Introduction to *A History of English Literature*, by E. Legouis and L. Cazamian.

    'Tennyson in 1833.' (*The Times Lit. Suppl.*, 14 Sept.) Reprinted in *The Poet as Citizen*, 1934.

1934.   *The Poet as Citizen, and Other Papers.*

  a. *Felicities of Thomas Traherne*, with an Introduction.

    Two Epigrams: 'To Cynthia' and 'The Chrysalis.' (*The Spectator*, 23 Nov.)

1935. *a.* *English Sonnets*, a New and Enlarged Edition.

    'A Brief Ode for May the 6th.' (*Chanticlere*, Easter Term, revised from *The Cambridge Review*, 10 May.)

    'The Scholarly Don.' (*Time and Tide*, 23 Feb.)

1935.   Introduction to The 'Johanna Maria', translated by B. W. Downs from the Dutch of A. van Schendel.

Introduction to Essays in Cornish History, by Charles Henderson, edited by A. L. Rowse and M. I. Henderson.

'Sea Stories: a Chance Catalogue.' (The Times Lit. Suppl., 15 Aug.)

'Consultants to Admiration', a Review of The New Book of English Verse. (The Observer, 3 Nov.)

1936.   Introduction to Thirty-one Poems from the Spenser Society of Cambridge University.

Introduction to Seas and Shores of England, by Edmund Vale.

'In Memoriam, King George V.' (The Cambridge Review, 24 Jan.)

Addresses to Queen Mary and King Edward VIII, written for the University of Cambridge. (Cambridge University Reporter, 21 April.)

Two Epigrams: 'A Garden Speaks' and 'On the Cnidian Venus.' (The Spectator, 1 May.)

'Monuments.' (14 lines of verse, The Cambridge Review, 10 June.)

'English in the United States', a Review of The American Language, by H. L. Mencken. (Sunday Times, 4 Aug.)

'Step o' One Side.' ('The Times' Weekly Edition, 12 Nov.) (Short story.) Reprinted in Mystery Stories, 1937.

Obituary of Gustave David. (The Cambridge Review, 27 Nov.) Reprinted in David of Cambridge, 1937.

1937.   Mystery Stories: Twenty Stories from the Works of Sir Arthur Quiller-Couch.

David of Cambridge: Some Appreciations, by T. R. Glover, Q, W. H. D. Rouse, H. F. Stewart, and S. C. Roberts.

This Sceptred Isle: a Children's Masque performed at Place, Fowey, on the Coronation Day of King George VI.

Introduction to Kings and Heroes, Verses by Erica Fay.

Introduction to Chinese Lyrics, translated by Ch'u Ta-kao.

'Unlocking the Bible,' a Review of The Bible Designed to be Read as Literature. (The Observer, 24 Oct.)

'Faithful Jane, a Christmas Story.' (The Times, 24 Dec.)

1938.   Introduction to The Wrath of Achilles, translated from The Iliad by S. O. Andrew.

1939. a.   The Oxford Book of English Verse 1250–1918.

1940.   'Sursum Corda.' (12 lines of verse, The Times, 1 June.)

Introduction to Byron, Poetry and Prose, edited by D. Nichol Smith.

Introduction to The Spell of Oxford, a Book of Photographs, by S. W. Colyer.

1941.   Introduction to Cornish Tales, by Charles Lee.

1941. Review of *The New Testament in Basic English*. (*The Cambridge Review*, 6 June.)

1942 'To an Old Leader.' (10 lines of verse, *The Cambridge Review*, 31 Oct.)

1943. *Cambridge Lectures*. ('Everyman's Library.') (13 lectures selected from previous volumes.)

'Sixty Years of *The Oxford Magazine*.' (*The Oxford Magazine*, 21 Jan.)

Review of *The Daily Press*, by H. Wilson Harris. (*The Cambridge Review*, 5 June.)

1944. *Shorter Stories*. (28 stories selected by Q from previous volumes.)

Memories and Opinions, an Unfinished Autobiography, edited with an Introduction by S. C. Roberts.

'On Basic English: a Challenge to Innovators.' (*The Times Lit. Suppl.*, 30 Sept.),

1945. Introduction to *Cornwall and its People*, by A. K. H. Jenkin.

NOT YET PUBLISHED

n. *Castle d'Or*. (Unfinished.)

Introduction to *Chaucer's Canterbury Tales Re-spelled, Adapted, and Annotated for the Modern Reader*, by the Hon. Gilbert Coleridge.

The Two Householders, a Play in One Act (from his short story in *I Saw Three Ships*).

INDEX

Index

Index

Index

Index